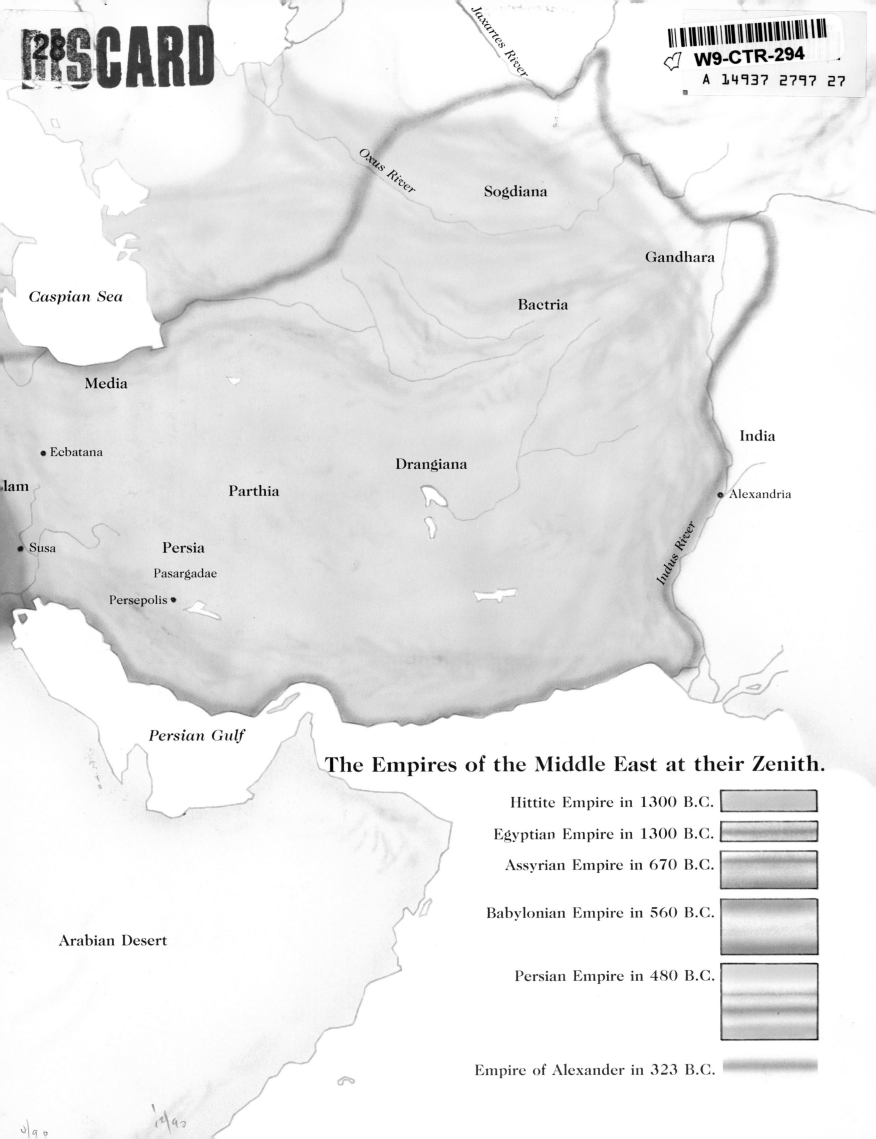

Juxartes River

Oxus River

Sogdiana

Gandhara

Bactria

Caspian Sea

Media

India

Ecbatana

Drangiana

lam

Parthia

Alexandria

Indus River

Susa

Persia

Pasargadae

Persepolis

Persepolis •

Persian Gulf

The Empires of the Middle East at their Zenith.

Hittite Empire in 1300 B.C.

Egyptian Empire in 1300 B.C.

Assyrian Empire in 670 B.C.

Babylonian Empire in 560 B.C.

Persian Empire in 480 B.C.

Arabian Desert

Empire of Alexander in 323 B.C.

Series director: Michel Pierre, Professor of History
Art Director: Giampiero Caiti
Assistant art director: Christine Tonglet
Editor: Martine Prosper
Project editor for U.S. edition: Joanne Fink
Editor for U.S. edition: Ruth Marsh
English text consultant: Walter O. Moeller, Senior Professor,
  Temple University.
Maps: Michael Welply
Photographs: Cassochrome, C.G.V. and Wespin under the technical
  direction of Claude Duhem.

The publisher would like to thank the following individuals and organizations for their assistance in the preparation of this book: Jean-Pierre Adam of the Bureau d'Architecture du C.N.R.S., Miss Gosselin of the Sous-Direction de l'Archéologie in Paris, the Turkish Bureau of Tourism in Paris, the Egyptian Office of Tourism in Paris, the Musée Borély in Marseilles and the Department of Egyptian Antiquities at the Musée du Louvre.

Picture credits

Collection Albert Kahn: pages 8, 9, 24. Artephot/Nimattallah: pages 10, 17 (l). Artephot/Babey: pages 12 (2 ph.), 13 (t), 26. Artephot/Kumasegawa: page 19. Artephot/Roland: page 55. Artephot/Musée de Xian: pages 58, 68/69, 69 (b). Artephot/Robert Harding Picture Library, London: pages 68, 69 (t). Artephot/Percheron: page 70 (t). Artephot: page 70 (b). Giraudon: pages 13, 30 35(r), 38, 50, 54, 71. Lauros-Giraudon: 72 (t). Réunion des Musées nationaux: pages 15, 27 (t), 28, 41, 42, 45, 46, 48 (b), 57. Bildarchiv Preussischer Kulturbesitz/Jürgen Liepe: page 17 (r). Michel Pierre: pages 20, 22, 23. Egyptian Collection of Musée Borély, Marseille: page 27 (b). Musée du Louvre-Egyptian Antiquities (Ph. M. Chuzeville); page 29. Turkish Bureau of Tourism: pages 34, 35 (l). A.A.A. Photo/Naud: page 48 (t). A.A.A. Photo/Marthelot: page 77. Bertrand Coblence: page 53. Guilheim Fabre: pages 60, 62. Magnum/Erich Lessing: page 67. Collection Viollet: pages 73 (2 ph.), 75. Roger-Viollet: page 74. Jean-Pierre Adam: page 72.

Library of Congress Cataloging-in-Publication Data

Chadefaud, Catherine.
  [Premiers empires. English]
  The first empires/Catherine Chadefaud, with the assistance of Jean-Michel Coblence; English translation by Anthea Ridett; illustrations by Michel Tarride, Christian Maucler, and Véronique Ageorges.
    p. cm.—(The Human story)
  Translation of: Les premiers empires.
  Bibliography: p.
  Includes index.
  Summary: Describes the earliest civilizations of Egypt, Asia and the area between the Mediterranean and the Persian Gulf.
  ISBN 0-382-09481-6
  1. Middle East—Civilization—To 622—Juvenile literature.
  2. Asia—Civilization—Juvenile literature. [1. Middle East—Civilization—to 622. 2. Asia—Civilization.] I. Coblence, Jean-Michel. II. Tarride, Michel, ill. III. Maucler, Christian, ill.
IV. Ageorges, Véronique, ill. V. Title. VI. Series: Histoire des hommes. English.
DS57.C4613 1987
939.4—dc19   87-22707

THE HUMAN STORY

THE FIRST EMPIRES

Catherine Chadefaud
with the assistance of
Jean-Michel Coblence
English translation by Anthea Ridett
Illustrations by Michel Tarride,
Christian Maucler, and
Véronique Ageorges

Silver Burdett Press

Englewood Cliffs, New Jersey

CONTENTS

PREFACE

Strengthened by their farmers, their priests, their scribes, and their armies, some peoples of Asia began to flex their muscles and dream of conquest. They did not limit their ambitions to nearby cities and kingdoms; the new conquerors traveled over mountains, deserts, and sometimes the oceans. They proclaimed themselves Pharaoh, King of Kings, Son of the Sky, and Blessed of the Gods.

To impress their subjects and inspire fear in their enemies, they built splendid cities, with massive walls and ever larger temples. Sometimes, drunk with glory and dreaming of immortality, they built their own final resting places as if they themselves were gods.

Every day the known world grew larger, the numbers of conquered nations increased, and the riches to be gained became ever more tempting. And, while the empires were expanding, the memory of the past took lasting form. In China, India, and Egypt the first historians retold in epic works the tales of legendary deeds performed by those whom the gods protected.

But what warfare could achieve, warfare could also undo. At the borders of these empires pranced the steeds of the barbarians, their riders hungry for pillage, destroyers who would become empire builders themselves. And very often neighboring empires clashed in merciless struggles that sometimes lasted for centuries. There were, too, some vain attempts by rulers to establish dynasties that were designed to last for hundreds of generations. But these were short-lived and crumbled in two decades.

Little is left of Babylon, Persepolis, Pataliputra, Memphis, Luoyang, and Nineveh. Only a few sandy hillocks and some pillars remain. But they are reminders of great civilizations whose rulers dreamed great dreams for the benefit of humanity as well as their own glory.

THE ANNUAL FLOOD

Every year the Nile flooded its banks. Every year the Egyptians gave thanks to the gods for the return of the waters that fertilized their land.

Slowly the river level would rise, covering the land right up to the edges of the first houses, which were built prudently some distance from the river bank. Then, after several weeks, the waters would begin to fall back, leaving behind a layer of mud rich in fertile silt. It was called *keme*, "the black land." The ideogram, or picture symbol, that the scribes used to represent it took the form of a clod of earth with grass and irises growing from it. In sharp contrast to *keme* was *dashre*, "the red land." This refers to the sterile desert tract around the curves of the river, between the Fourth Cataract, or waterfall, and the Delta leading to the sea.

Everything revolved around the annual flood: the rhythm of life, the labor in the fields, fishing, wildfowling in the marshes, and the great building projects. It was the flood that divided the year into three seasons of four months each. The first was *akhet*, "the flood-time." This was followed by the months of *peret*, when the earth made its reappearance, still moist with its covering of silt. The last season of the year was *shemu*, the "harvest," the time for reaping the barley, wheat, and flax.

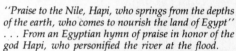

"Praise to the Nile, Hapi, who springs from the depths of the earth, who comes to nourish the land of Egypt" . . . *From an Egyptian hymn of praise in honor of the god Hapi, who personified the river at the flood.*

The Egyptians had no idea where the source of the Nile was, nor did they have an explanation for the annual flooding. The Nile waters actually rise in two separate branches known as the Blue Nile, which crosses Ethiopia, and the White Nile, which starts in Lake Victoria in Central Africa. The real source of the river is the Kagera River, a tributary of Lake Victoria.

At flood time, the irrigation canals and ditches filled up with water. In the fall, the dikes were breached to allow the muddy waters, swollen with fertile silt, to spread over the land before it was plowed and sown.

WORKING THE LAND

After each annual flood, workers dug through the silt-covered earth to remove stones, pebbles, and dead wood washed up by the waters. Then, supervised by scribes, they had to mark out afresh the various plots of land. Egypt may well have been, in the words of the Greek historian Herodotus, ''the gift of the Nile,'' but it was paid for by a great deal of hard work.

Methods of working the soil were all based on a very ancient system of irrigation. To make the most of the silt-laden floodwaters, the peasants dug and maintained a network of canals, separated by earthen dikes, on either side of the Nile. During the flood, the canals were opened, to be closed again as soon as the waters reached maximum height. The checkerboard of fields could then be drained or irrigated as needed during the rest of the year. It was a complicated system in which every member of the village community had to play a part.

The soil was first hoed and then tilled by ox-drawn plows. Then the laborers sowed wheat, barley (the first cereal to be cultivated in Egypt), and flax from which linen clothes would be made. At harvest time, men and women reaped the crops, using bronze-bladed sickles and making up the sheafs with care; the straw went to feed the animals.

Officially, no one could own land or herds apart from the pharaoh and the high priests, who were allowed to receive gifts from their lord. So the peasants cultivated the land almost entirely for the profit of the state, and had to provide their labor free. However, there were ways of getting around the law; some of the top civil servants, for instance, were given land in payment for their services, in addition to their salaries. And from there it was only a small step to regarding themselves as true landowners.

The art of growing grapevines on trellises had existed since ancient times, well before the pyramids. The Egyptian word for vine, kerem, originated in Asia. But it is not known for certain whether vines were imported to Egypt. Most paintings depict red grapes; they were grown in the gardens and orchards of temples and private houses. There the Egyptians could enjoy the shade of the swaying trellises, planted among fig, date, and pomegranate trees.

Little is known about Egyptian methods of winemaking. Some vintages were blended and flavored with honey and spices. It is known they were made with a great deal of care, and harvests were large for those days. One inscription refers to 20 vine growers delivering 1,200 jugs of ''good wine,'' 50 jugs of alcohol, and 50 jugs of ordinary table wine. The Egyptians improved the quality of their produce by importing vinestocks from Syria. During the Greek period, they were still exporting several of their famous wines throughout the whole of the Mediterranean basin.

The peasants stocked up on food supplies by hunting and especially by fishing, depending on where they lived. The marshes contained a plentiful supply of fish, which were caught in nets from boats made of papyrus reeds. There, too, the Egyptians hunted migratory birds that sought shelter in the reed thickets, as shown here in this painting from the New Kingdom. Two dangerous animals sometimes hid among the reeds, the hippopotamus and the crocodile. People also made trips to the edges of the desert to hunt antelopes, gazelles, and the oryx. The king and his courtiers enjoyed lion-hunting in the desert. (Egyptian Museum, Turin).

Egypt's agriculture enabled the country to be self-sufficient. According to the papyrus texts of the New Kingdom period (Eighteenth–Twentieth Dynasties), a normal yield of cereals consisted of twenty sheaves to the acre, which was higher than anywhere else in the ancient world. When it became a Roman province in 30 B.C., Egypt was treated as the granary of Rome.

Egypt, "the gift of the Nile,"
was won at the price of ceaseless toil.

WOOD, BRICK, AND GOLD

As the festival of the New Year drew close, the carpenters, painters, and goldsmiths in the workrooms attached to the great temple of Ammon at Thebes would be hard at work in preparation for the royal minister's visit of inspection. Around them stood chests inlaid with ebony from the land of Nubia, carved cedar armchairs from Lebanon, chalices made of gold and lapis lazuli, the blue stone that decorated so many of the pharaoh's bracelets and breastpieces called pectorals. These skilled craftsmen passed down the secrets of their trade from generation to generation. Remarkable jewels, like those found in Tutankhamen's tomb, were first made in the age of the pyramids. A golden crown, once belonging to Queen Hetepheres, has flowers and leaves of the most intricate design. Lucky charms, called amulets, made of faience (Egyptian pottery) and glazed with turquoise, have also been found dating back to those ancient times.

There were no independent craftsmen in Egypt; every worker was employed either by the royal administration or by the temple priests, who were powerful and numerous throughout the land. Their wages were paid in goods instead of money and were based on the qualifications and responsibilities of each member of the team. Prisoners of war made up a small body of slaves, who were sent to work in the mines and quarries. The quarrymen and miners had the task of extracting the raw materials needed for the royal building works. They were sent to distant sites for several months of the year, accompanied by foremen, soldiers to protect the sites from looters, and sailors who supervised the loading of the cargoes on the Nile. There were gold mines at Wadi Hammamat in the south, alabaster quarries at Hatnub, the sandstone quarries of Gebel Silsila, and the quarries of pink granite at Aswan. Sometimes journeys were made to the turquoise mines of the Sinai, to bring back the *mejkat*, highly prized for its use in inlay work and jewelry. All the raw materials were taken to the Nile and carried from there by boat to the workshops of the towns. A careful inventory was taken before they were handed out to the craftsmen.

Stone was used only for temples and tombs, the "houses of eternity." All of the other buildings, particularly dwelling houses, were made of wood, straw, or mud bricks. The masons made these bricks from the thick Nile mud, mixed with straw and poured into wooden molds to be dried in the sun. But bricks and wood do not easily withstand the passage of time. Apart from a few remnants at Kahun and Amarna, the towns of ancient Egypt have totally vanished.

Woodworking was the province of the joiner and the carpenter. Together, they often chose the types of wood to be used for particular purposes. The roofs of houses were made with palm-tree beams. Sycamore, acacia, tamarind, and pine were used to make furniture and everyday objects. The best wood for boat building was the durable cedar imported from Lebanon. And to create fine inlays, the joiner obtained ebony from the Cush region of Nubia.

This pectoral was worn by Sesostris III (1887–1849 B.C.), whose first name is written inside the cartouche, the frame in the center. Made of gold, semiprecious stones, and vitreous paste, it was both a breast decoration and a protective amulet. At the top, in its claws a royal vulture holds the rings of shem, *symbols of eternity. On either side of the cartouche, a sphinx with a falcon's head crowned with plumes tramples underfoot Egypt's enemies, the Nubians and Asians. (Cairo Museum)*

Women preparing rushes. Rushes were woven to make baskets and mats. Many of these goods have been found intact inside tombs. Some still contain the remnants of offerings of flowers, fruits, and vegetables.

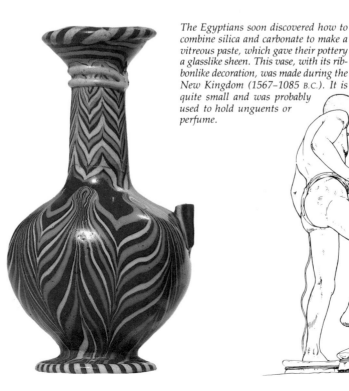

The Egyptians soon discovered how to combine silica and carbonate to make a vitreous paste, which gave their pottery a glasslike sheen. This vase, with its ribbonlike decoration, was made during the New Kingdom (1567–1085 B.C.). It is quite small and was probably used to hold unguents or perfume.

Two joiners finishing off a wooden casket. Sycamore was the wood most often used for this, but cedar was better because it lasted longer. While one of the craftsmen removes the last shavings, his helper is smoothing off the carved face. The casket will then be painted.

A large number of miniature hippopotamuses in blue faience, about 4½ inches long, have been found in the tombs of the Twelfth Dynasty (2000–1849 B.C.). They were decorated with paintings of marsh plants (flags), a type of grass called Potamogeton lucens, and water lilies. They may have been used in magical rites as a protection against the dangers of the marshes. (Louvre Museum)

This golden bowl belonging to Thutmose III is a beautiful example of the goldsmith's art at the beginning of the fifteenth century B.C. (Louvre Museum)

A carpenter trying to split a palm-tree beam, which will probably form part of a roof. It was hard work because the saw, like most tools, was made of bronze. Other tools, such as T-squares and levels, have been found in tombs.

The heat around the smiths' furnace is hardly bearable. One of the three men is keeping the fire going by working bellows with his feet. The others are holding over the furnace a kind of mold in which metal will be melted. At the right, a tanner is preparing leather, which his helper is making up into sandals. Most leather was made from sheepskin, but sometimes the hides of cows and gazelles were used. They were cut up, thoroughly cleaned, and then greased.

THE LIFE
OF THE SCRIBES

First by drawing pictures, then by using certain signs for specific sounds, the ancient Egyptians learned to write. The invention of writing was probably the most important event in ancient Egyptian history. It was the scribes who were entrusted with the teaching of this precious art. The scribes' training schools were known as "Houses of Life." In a huge chamber near the Temple of Ammon, seated on a rush mat, the pupil would cut a reed, dip it in a bowl of ink, and listen to the master's instructions as he made his first attempts at writing. It took a long time to become proficient at drawing a vulture, or the fine outlines of a reed. The beginner had to practice at first on *ostraka*, pieces of broken pottery, before he was allowed to work on papyrus, an expensive material not to be wasted. He copied ancient texts over and over.

Because reading and writing were highly valued skills, scribes were greatly respected by all. Their calling demanded great diligence, perseverance, and attention to detail. The Houses of Life were always situated in towns near a temple, and they included several departments and grades. During the first few years, the young pupil learned the basics of writing, reading, and arithmetic: the single Egyptian word *seh* stood for the activities of both writing and drawing. The pupil also had to learn how to write in an elegant style, train his memory to retain all the ideograms, and grasp the subtleties of grammatical construction.

Pupils with natural gifts in particular areas were encouraged to specialize. One might become an artist, drawing the illustrations to texts; another might become an accountant in the temple offices. A third might be assigned to work alongside a building foreman, in order to become an architect. This was the case with the royal architect Imhotep, who built the Step Pyramid for Pharaoh Djoser, and Senmut, who was in charge of building the temple at Deir al-Bahri commissioned by Queen Hatshepsut. After working his way up through the different grades, a competent scribe could aspire to becoming a royal administrator in the provinces, and from there advance his career to the highest posts in central government.

Aside from these few famous names, a large number of ordinary scribes were assigned to work in the organization of the army. They looked after the commissariat, a branch of the army that provided food and supplies for the troops, and kept the accounts. There was also another kind of elite, who worked in the secret, enclosed atmosphere of the temple libraries. These were the scribes who copied the sacred texts. Among them were theological experts whose task was to interpret rites and beliefs whose meaning had become obscure over the course of time. They were the last to hold the keys to the hieroglyphs; during the Greek period they continued to write long theological discourses on the walls of the temples built by the Ptolemaic kings, at Idfu and Dendera. Their knowledge was lost when the Roman emperor Theodosius closed down all the pagan temples in 395 B.C., and the meaning of the hieroglyphs was erased from Egyptian memory. It was not until the nineteenth century, when the French scholar Jean-François Champollion went to Egypt, that the inscriptions the scribes had so carefully copied for the gods recovered their meaning.

Papyrus making
The stalk of the papyrus reed, which grew in the marshes, was chopped into sections and the outer rind removed. The sections were then split into narrow strips, using a bronze-bladed cutter, which were cut into lengths about 16 inches long. They were hammered flat with a wooden mallet, then laid side by side and covered with a second layer at right angles to the first. These layers were then glued together with gum arabic to form a sheet, which was again hammered to meld them together. This was pasted to other sheets made in the same fashion, to make a roll of papyrus up to a yard and a half long. It could then be used to write on. The text was written in black and titles and headings in red. On some documents, spaces were left for small color illustrations. This is how the book of the Scribe Nebked was written; an extract from it is shown above. Dating from the Eighteenth Dynasty, it is known as the Book of the Dead, and is preserved in the Louvre Museum in Paris.

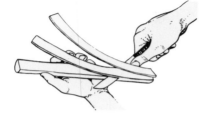

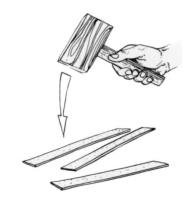

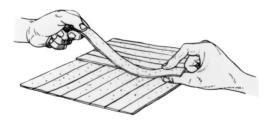

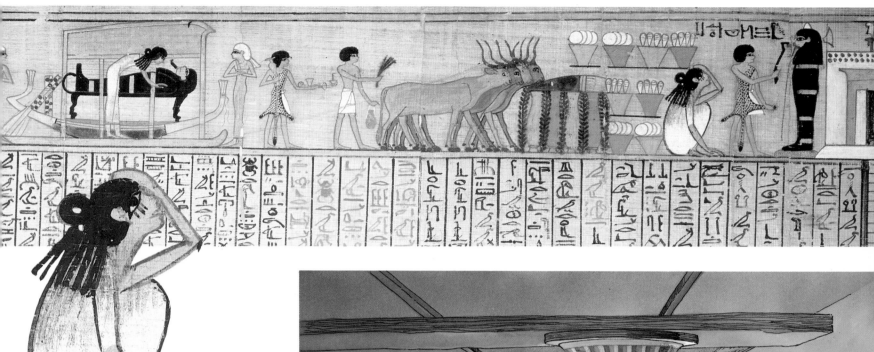

In this dimly lit schoolroom, little boys are learning to copy the ancient texts. Texts called Sebayt, "wisdom literature," were packed with moral advice from sages to the young. One of them praised the merits of the silent man who knows at once how to listen, hear, and obey: in the Egyptian language there was only one verb for all three activities. This is no consolation to the pupil at the left, who is being threatened with a beating. Egyptian masters didn't spare the rod. At the far end of the room the schoolmaster has placed a chest filled with papyrus scrolls, ready for the next lesson. The pupils will have to copy the wise words of the pharaohs and lists of difficult geographical terms, while the more advanced will be studying mathematics—calculating the surface of a triangular field and adding up fractions.

For those who are already well versed in grammar and the range of ideograms, one exercise consists of writing essays in the form of letters to an imaginary correspondent, in which they must include as many scholarly and unusual words as they can.

LORD OF
TWO KINGDOMS

In its early history, Egypt was called "the land of the two kingdoms." The two kingdoms were Lower Egypt, situated in the north on the Nile Delta, and Upper Egypt, which extended along the river from the Delta to the First Cataract at Aswan.

Tradition has it that at the beginning of the third millennium B.C. the country was unified by Menes, king of Upper Egypt, when he imposed his rule over the people of Lower Egypt. Thus Menes founded the first of the thirty dynasties of pharaohs who were to rule Egypt for nearly three thousand years. From then on Pharaoh Menes was "Lord of Two Kingdoms." Later this unification would be commemorated in public by his wearing the Double Crown, consisting of the red crown of Lower Egypt encased within the white crown of its conqueror, Upper Egypt.

The entire pharaonic system of Egypt was based on the idea of a divine ruler. The pharaoh was not simply the guardian of the gods' earthly possessions: his kingship made him a member of their world. On him depended the ordering of the world, the rhythm of the seasons, the cycle of days and nights, and the rise of the Nile. In his hands he held two symbols of his divine status, both emblems of the god Osiris—the *heka*, the crook used by shepherds to guide their flocks, and the *flagellum*, a kind of small whip. Another symbol sometimes adopted by pharaohs was a small false beard, in imitation of the beards of the gods. It can be seen in some of the pharaohs' portraits—including those of Queen Hatshepsut! And of course the pharaoh was immortal; the pyramid tombs were built for him to dwell in for all eternity.

The pharaoh's power was absolute. With his chief minister, the vizier, at his side, he controlled a powerful centralized administration, supported by a large and efficient bureaucracy. The legal owner of all Egypt, the pharaoh also directed the country's economic activity. Peasants and craftsmen, merchants and sailors, all were his servants. And of course he was also supreme military commander and the high priest of the temples, "the first prophet."

The pharaoh's life, lived on the fringes of the ordinary human world, was full of pomp and ceremony. On state occasions he distributed golden collars as a mark of royal favor to his faithful servants. When he appeared before his people, he wore a golden pectoral overlaid with vitreous paste (porcelain enamel) or precious stones. Religious hymns and official texts all celebrated this vision, half man, half god. Sometimes, however, looking through a literary text, we glimpse quite a different image. In *The Story of Sinuhe* the author portrays the ruler as having very human qualities. He is at times firm and courageous, at others gentle and generous. The story *King Khufu and the Magician* portrays the pharaoh in his leisure hours, and some bas-reliefs show him relaxing unceremoniously in the bosom of his family. In the grand, eternal figurehead of the pharaoh, it seems that the Egyptians had a good understanding of the difference between the man and his role.

The Festival of Heb-Sed
At the beginning of the Third Dynasty, Pharaoh Djoser commissioned his architect, Imhotep, to build a group of chapels around the Step Pyramid of Sakkarah, where he could celebrate the festival of Heb-Sed in full glory. This festival, which was celebrated in the thirtieth year of the pharaoh's reign (or in late pharaonic times when he felt it was necessary) was definitely a very important ritual by which the king renewed his powers. At Sakkarah, several of the chapels have a very curious appearance. They are built in limestone to look like reed houses; they are the same shape, and their pillars and walls are carved to look like the bundles of reeds and rush matting that served as pillars and wall coverings in Egyptian houses. Even stranger is the fact that they are not real buildings; they consist only of facades, built against solid walls, like theatrical scenery to be seen only from the front. It seems that here the Pharaoh took part in a ritual by running around the perimeter in memory of a sacred act performed by one of his ancestors. Long after the Old Kingdom, other rulers were depicted as taking part in this festival. According to some inscriptions, Ramses II, who ruled for sixty-seven years, celebrated this festival fourteen times.

More than once Egyptian queens became rulers in their own right—that is, they were pharaohs. The most famous of these were Hatshepsut, who ruled in the Eighteenth Dynasty, and Cleopatra, who was the last ruler of an independent Egypt. Even when not direct rulers, they were the carriers of the right to rule. For this reason, the Great Wife of the King usually was his own sister or a close relative. Thus, like Nefertiti, they left a deep impression on Egyptian history. She was married to Akhenaten (Amenophis IV) and actively shared the rule with her husband. Her name means "The Beautiful One Has Come." How appropriate! (Egyptian Museum, Berlin)

At the Pharaoh's side, Nefertiti became a devotee of the new worship of Aten, the universal god, represented by the sun's disk. The king overthrew the too-powerful priests of Ammon, traditional ruler of the gods, and changed his own name to Akhenaten, "Serviceable to the Aten." Nefertiti left Thebes with him and they went to live at the new capital of Akhetaten ("The Horizon of the Aten," now Tell al Amarna). When Nefertiti was widowed in 1354 B.C. she seems to have remained faithful to the worship of Aten and retired to the palace of Amarna, while Ammon's priests plotted to restore the traditional worship of Thebes and mutilated the dead pharaoh's monuments.

There are many statues of the pharaohs, which played a part in political life and royal propaganda. Some of them are huge. The pharaoh, who was the mediator of the gods, had to inspire awe and fear in his subject peoples. This statue of Ramses II (who ruled from 1304 to 1237 B.C.) is over 8 feet high. However, the manner in which it is carved expresses the humanity, generosity, and stability of the power it stands for. The king is carrying the attributes of his position; he is crowned with a képresh, or war crown, probably to remind people that he brought about peace by crushing the Hittites. The inscriptions on his garments repeat the list of his glorious titles. And on the base of the throne beneath his sandaled feet can be seen all the enemies he defeated for the benefit of the "Two Kingdoms" and to ensure the survival of maat—the correct balance of the universe and of Egypt, ordered according to the will of the gods. (Egyptian Museum, Turin)

THE PHARAOH'S ARMIES

E arly in Egypt's history, during the days of the Old Kingdom, the provincial militias were enough to ensure the safety of the territory and the safe transport of Nubian ebony, gold, and ivory. But Egypt's geographical position made it vulnerable and eventually a permanent army had to be organized, well-trained, and well-armed, to protect its wealth and territory.

Egypt was particularly vulnerable in the south, the route most often taken by nomads from Asia who made regular raids against the Delta. It was from the south that the Hyksos invaded on horseback in 1720 B.C.. They overran the Nile Valley and introduced to Egypt the arts of horsemanship and chariot driving.

In the face of this threat, the Egyptians built a chain of fortresses and organized a series of "defensive" operations. These operations ended by becoming offensives. This was especially true during the period of the New Kingdom (1567–1085 B.C.), when Thutmose III led a number of military campaigns against both Asia in the northwest and Nubia in the south. Nubia was subdued, placed under the authority of a viceroy, and eventually became Egyptianized.

Thutmose also made conquests in the east. He went on to attack the powerful kingdom of Mitanni, in northwestern portion of Mesopotamia. This was a strategic move for from there the borders of neighboring Anatolia could be better guarded. But there another danger was looming—the Hittite Empire.

The small principalities of Syria and Palestine, already under Egyptian rule, were also threatened by the growing Hittite power. Together with Egypt, they built up a tight network of diplomatic agreements. The pharaoh set up a loose system of protectorates and alliances in these principalities, leaving the administration largely to the native princes, and respecting the local customs, languages, and religions. Egyptian rule took the form of commercial treaties and the imposing of an annual tribute of produce and military duties.

Thus protected and consolidated as an empire, Egypt enjoyed a period of prosperity during the New Kingdom, which culminated in the long reign of Ramses II (1304–1237 B.C.). The Asiatic conquests scarcely survived him. After the Battle of Kadesh, Egypt was forced to share Syria with the Hittites, and Ramses's reign saw the end of Egypt's sole domination over the East. But its cultural influences remained. Many Egyptian or Egyptian-style objects have been found at Palestinian and Syrian sites, such as Ugarit, Byblos, Askelon, and Beth Shan. Isis was still worshiped, as well as Baal and Astarte.

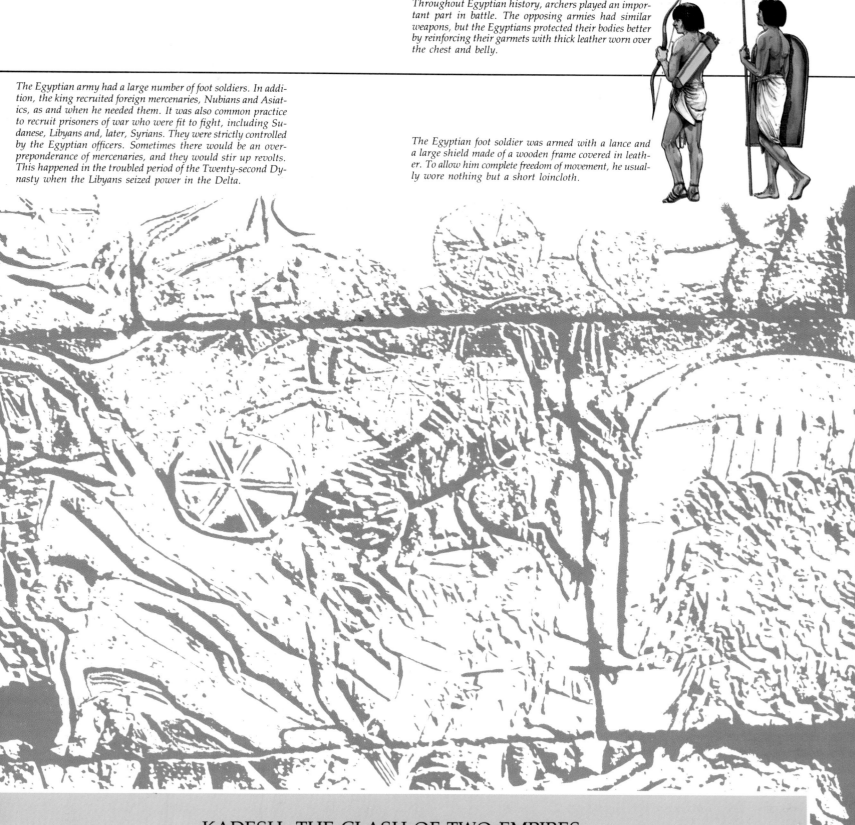

Throughout Egyptian history, archers played an important part in battle. The opposing armies had similar weapons, but the Egyptians protected their bodies better by reinforcing their garments with thick leather worn over the chest and belly.

The Egyptian army had a large number of foot soldiers. In addition, the king recruited foreign mercenaries, Nubians and Asiatics, as and when he needed them. It was also common practice to recruit prisoners of war who were fit to fight, including Sudanese, Libyans and, later, Syrians. They were strictly controlled by the Egyptian officers. Sometimes there would be an overpreponderance of mercenaries, and they would stir up revolts. This happened in the troubled period of the Twenty-second Dynasty when the Libyans seized power in the Delta.

The Egyptian foot soldier was armed with a lance and a large shield made of a wooden frame covered in leather. To allow him complete freedom of movement, he usually wore nothing but a short loincloth.

KADESH: THE CLASH OF TWO EMPIRES

In the fifth year of his reign, Ramses II left Egypt with his troops organized in four corps. The standards (flags) dedicated to the gods fluttered in the wind as the soldiers marched alongside the marshes of the eastern delta and thrust into the desert on the Palestinian side.

The king reached Syria at the Orontes River, where he believed the Hittites were massed, to the north of the fortress of Kadesh. But he had been given false information by spies in the pay of the Hittites; believing the enemy to be farther away than they were, Ramses advanced on Kadesh with only his horse chariots and the first corps. Just as he was setting up camp, the Hittites made a ferocious surprise attack.

Unable to wait for the rest of the army to arrive, the king and his soldiers threw themselves into the fray in the face of 2,500 enemy chariots. The fighting was fierce.

Muwatallis, the Hittite king, was unable to exploit his advantage of surprise to the full, for he too was waiting for reinforcements from his allies. The battle ended with no victory on either side—despite the claims of the Egyptian scribes who recorded the event!

In 1284 B.C. Ramses and Khattusilis III, Muwatallis's successor, signed the first alliance treaty in history, delineating the areas of each country's influence and promising lasting peace between the two nations.

THE SACRED TEMPLES

Every year, when the annual flood was at its height and the great city of Thebes slumbered in the heavy heat and dust, it was time to celebrate the Festival of Ope. Every year townsfolk and villagers waited impatiently for the priests to bring the image of the god Ammon out of the temple in a wooden barge and carry it with all due ceremony to the Nile. There it was placed on a splendid barge, which traveled slowly upriver, escorted by hundreds of boats carrying worshipers. The god was taken to the Temple at Luxor, on the east bank of the Nile, where Ammon made a triumphal entrance in the midst of libations, the smoke of incense, music, and dancing. These great festivals were very special occasions for the worshipers, since they were not allowed to enter the temples and had few opportunities to be near the images of the gods. At Luxor the celebrations went on for nearly twenty days, after which the crowd, happy and content, accompanied the god and his priests back to their home at Karnak.

Egypt had a great many gods and goddesses, each with their own hierarchical priesthood and temple and property. The priests did not live apart from the ordinary people. On the contrary, they all had families, and some followed their own occupations in the nearby town or village, visiting the temple during periods of service on a rotating basis.

In spite of the huge temples and written records of religious rituals, very little is known about Egyptian religion. Although it is difficult today to conceive of a people really believing in gods that were portrayed as half human, half animal, or bird, the Egyptians were sincere in their beliefs. But the special reverence they gave to Ammon, the king of the gods, and during the reign of Akhenaten to the Aten, the sun-disk god, suggest that they were beginning to develop the concept of one god who was the creator of the world.

The huge pillars of the Temple of Luxor, 65 feet high, tower over the visitor like a forest of giant papyrus reeds. On an equally large scale are the tall obelisks, which represent the rays of the kindly sun that lights the earth each morning.

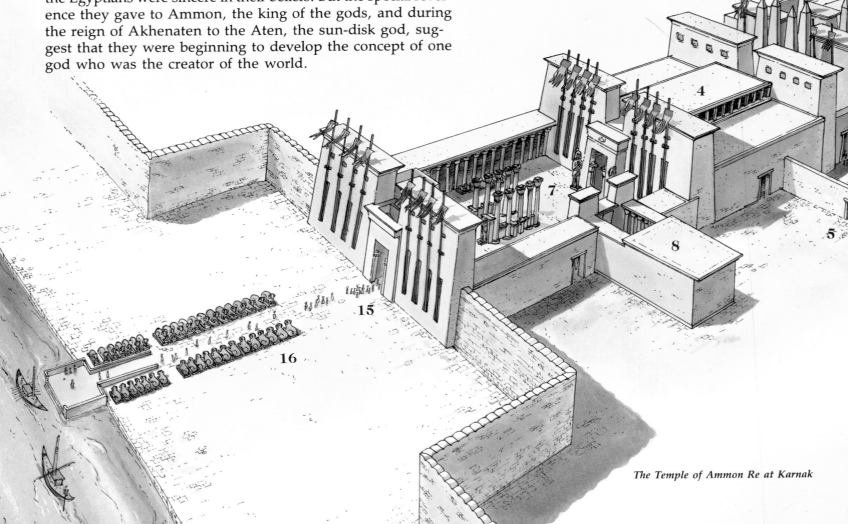

The Temple of Ammon Re at Karnak

The huge temple of Ammon Re stands at Karnak, once Ipet-Sut, about 370 miles from Cairo, and just north of ancient Thebes, a city the Greeks praised for its magnificence. The building of the temple began in the fifteenth century B.C. and it was continually added to and embellished from the New Kingdom period until Greco-Roman times. It stands on the right bank of the Nile, facing toward the Valley of the Kings and the grand tombs of the civil servants lying on the left bank. The complete temple has grown up around two main axes, or processional avenues—one leading to the Nile and ending at statues of winged sphinxes with rams' heads, the other leading to the south toward the Temple of Luxor, where river processions used to land bearing the image of the god Ammon.

Below is a reconstruction of the temple, with its various features numbered chronologically in the order in which they were built.

1. Site of the first Middle Kingdom temple.

2. The Akhmenu (Great Festival Hall) of Thutmose III.

3. The sacred lake. At certain festivals, Ammon's barge, the Ouserhat, floated on it.

4. The great Hypostyle Hall, 335 feet wide and 174 feet long. It was redecorated often. It contained 134 pillars standing like giant forest trees, the capitals (tops of the columns) ornamented with papyrus leaves. During the New Kingdom period, the inner and outer walls were decorated with bas-reliefs (low raised sculpture).

5. The "Court of the Cachette," lying between the third and seventh pylons (monumental gateways). Large numbers of sacred statues and vases from the New Kingdom period were uncovered here by French archaeologists.

6. A small chapel built by Amenophis II on the southern processional avenue (between the ninth and tenth pylons). Behind it can be seen the priests' houses.

7. The great temple courtyard, decorated during the New Kingdom period with pillars on each side and some colossal statues. At its north end stands the shrine built by Seti I for storing ceremonial wooden boats.

8. Temple built by Ramses III inside the great courtyard.

9. Courtyard between the eighth and ninth pylons. The eighth pylon was put up by Thutmose I. Several granite obelisks were added by Queen Hatshepsut (Eighteenth Dynasty). The ninth pylon was built under King Horemheb at the end of the Eighteenth Dynasty.

10. Site of the tenth and last pylon of the southern processional axis, built under Horemheb. Beyond it stands the temple of the goddess Mut, with a curious horsehose-shaped lake. Farther south stands the Temple of Luxor, where the processional route came to an end.

11. The fourth and fifth pylons, built under Thutmose I. Several granite obelisks were added by Queen Hatshepsut. Beyond them, to the east, lay a storeroom for sacred boats, which was rebuilt during the Greek era.

12. A building erected by King Taharqa during the Late Period, using materials from earlier buildings.

13. Speculative reconstruction of shops selling offerings, refurbished at different times.

14. The eastern gate was covered by mud bricks. Small chapels were built close by during the rule of the Ramesside pharaohs where oracles gave their decisions or opinions.

15. The first, or western, pylon, 371 feet long and 50 feet thick. As it now stands, it seems to date from Greek times. It was probably begun, but not finished, by the kings of the Bubastid Dynasty.

16. A walkway bordered with rams. This walkway probably led to a canal and a wharf, which gave access to the Nile at the times of the great processions.

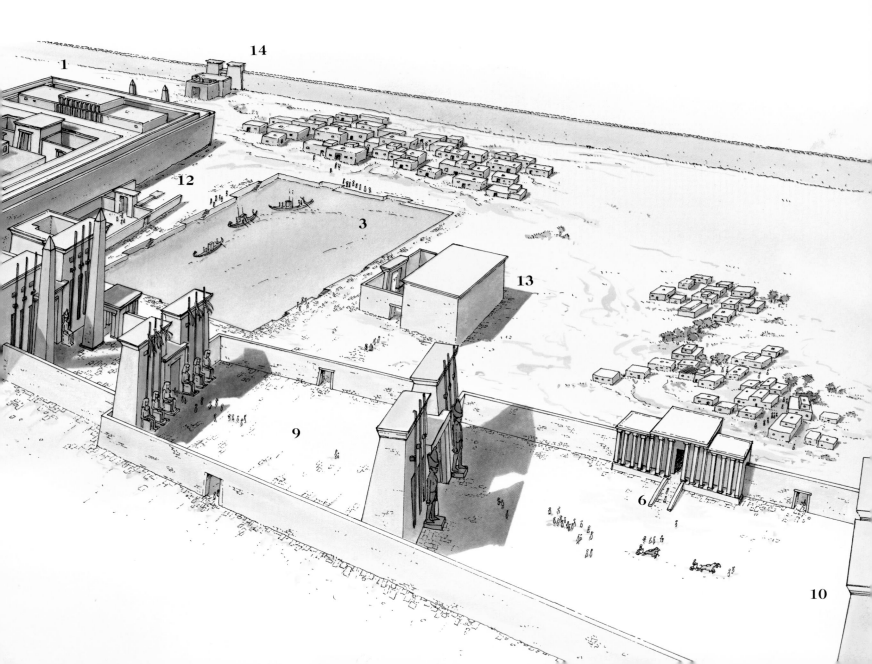

THE GREAT BUILDERS

In the third year of his reign (around 1152 B.C.), Ramses IV organized an extraordinary expedition to the Wadi Hammamat to bring back black granite, a valuable stone used specifically for tombs and statues. It was no small undertaking: the Hammamat was a three days' march from the Nile Valley, in the middle of the desert. Five thousand soldiers were mobilized, 110 officers, 200 temple builders, 50 officers of the law, 50 civil and temple servants, 20 army scribes, 2 of the king's personal attendants, 130 quarrymen and their assistants, 2 painters, 4 sculptors, 3 stone-cutting supervisors, an artistic supervisor, and finally the director of building works. The director was none other than the high priest of the Temple of Ammon, for whose benefit the whole operation was probably intended. In all, there were 8,368 men, provisioned by ten chariots, each drawn by six pairs of oxen—8,368 men for an expedition that was to last nearly three months. It is clear that when the pharaoh was planning a building, he did not believe in cutting corners.

The quarrymen's work was not limited to digging out stone. Once the blocks of stone had been taken out, they were cut on the spot to make their transport easier. But this was not always necessary. Some monuments were cut directly out of the rock face, like those of the tombs in the Valley of the Kings, the Abu Simbel temples, and the Great Sphinx at Giza. More usually, however, the enormous blocks of stone had to be carried dozens of miles, and causeways had to be built to take them from the quarries to the Nile. These causeways still exist. With the stones cleared from them piled up on each side, they are easy to recognize. The granite blocks were placed on wooden sledges and hundreds of workers hauled them along by hand. When they reached the banks of the Nile, they were hoisted onto barges, preferably at flood time, when the peasant labor force was available to help.

THE QUARRIES OF ASWAN

The Aswan quarries still retain the scars left by the wooden wedges that were inserted into the rocks to help detach the blocks of stone. These quarries were worked from the Old Kingdom onward, and provided the Egyptians with the beautiful pink granite from which they carved obelisks.

The quarry workers first removed any loose blocks and rolled them up the sides of the quarry on ramps of piled-up sand. When they had to cut a block from the rock, they chipped slots up to 12 inches deep around the shape they wanted, and then inserted wooden wedges into them. They soaked the wedges in water so that they expanded; then, aided by the extremes of day and night temperatures, the rock would ultimately split. When the process had been repeated several times, a block of granite could be removed. It was a crude method, and does not account for the extremely large blocks that were sometimes used. The lower temple of the Pyramid of Khafra contains blocks 180 cubic feet in size, each of which must weigh nearly 50 tons. It hardly seems possible that they could have been detached from the rock in this crude way.

It took a large work force to load and transport a 60-foot-long obelisk weighing around 220 tons. Sailors, with their rope-tying skills, were often brought in to help, in addition to the quarrymen and other laborers. The heavily laden barge was carried along by the river current, guided by ropes from dry land. Extra heavy barges were towed by several smaller boats.

HOUSES OF ETERNITY

On the edge of the Libyan Desert, the pyramids overhang the Nile Valley. Every morning at dawn they emerge from the mist rising from the river, ghostly shapes seeming to float above the palm trees, vast monuments which have fascinated travelers of every age. During the Islamic middle ages, they were identified as the granaries that Joseph, in the Bible story, built in preparation for the seven years of famine. Some people believed they concealed the pharaoh's wealth; one sultan even tried to open up the pyramid of Khufu to get at its treasure. Yet others have seen them as a center of esoteric culture, keys to the secret of the meaning of life. People have taken their measurements in order to discover the golden number on which their construction was based.

Most of the pyramids were built between the Third and the Sixth Dynasties (2780–2280 B.C.). Some were still being built during the Middle Kingdom, after a long period of troubles. Their shapes and the methods used to construct them changed as the centuries went by. The oldest was built for King Djoser, in the Third Dynasty. His architect, the scribe Imhotep, built the first great stone pyramid, now known as the Step Pyramid. The pyramid is made of a series of six *mastabas* (Arabic for ''bench''), shallow rectangular tombs, one on top of the other. Later, under the Fourth Dynasty rulers Khufu, Khafra, and Menkure, pyramids with triangular sides rising to a peak rose up on the plain of Giza. There were two exceptions: the bent pyramid (whose sides changed angles half way up) and the three-tiered pyramid, both built by King Snefu in the Fourth Dynasty.

How these gigantic monuments were built still remains something of a mystery. It is known that local peasants and craftsmen were conscripted to take part in the building, by a kind of forced labor system. Very early on, several organizations tried to free themselves from this obligation, and tables of immunity were drawn up exempting certain workers.

Pyramids were built by the ancient Egyptians as royal tombs, in preparation for their rulers' deaths. They were always part of an architectural complex. This complex included a lower temple in the valley, marking the entrance to the area and linked by a ramp to an upper temple where ritual offerings were made after the pharaoh's death. This sanctuary sprang to life after the royal funeral when the pyramid was finally sealed.

These great tombs give little indication of the life of the ruler after his death. Only the most recent, from the Fifth and Seventh Dynasties, contain instructions written on the inside walls, in the corridors down to the tomb and in the burial vault. These ''Pyramid Texts'' as they are known, were magical and religious formulas for protecting the king on his passage through the world of the gods. Like a divine falcon, the pharaoh would take flight, then he would board the boat of Re, the god of the sun, which renewed life every day for all eternity. The civil servants hoped that the king's immortality would rub off on them, and so they built their own tombs close by. Thus were born huge necropolises, or cemeteries. These Cities of the Dead, as they were known, reverberated with the sounds of the living who were appointed to look after them.

The immense 66-foot-high statue of the Sphinx at Giza is believed to be the image of King Khafra guarding the City of the Dead. Its strange appearance and enigmatic expression have given rise to much speculation. During the Middle Kingdom it was thought to be the god Harmachis, whose name means ''Horus who is on the horizon.'' Later it was identified with the Canaanite god Hurun. The Arabs of the Middle Ages gave it the name of Abu el-Hol, which means ''father of fear.''

Lying on the edges of the desert, it often became half buried in sand. A granite stele (monument) placed between its paws recounts how King Thutmose II, returning tired from the hunt, fell asleep in the Sphinx's shadow. In a dream, the ''god'' asked him to clear away the sand. This he did, and put up the stele to commemorate his deed. Napoleon Bonaparte, during his Egyptian campaign in 1798, also had the sand cleared away, hoping that it might conceal a secret entrance.

The pyramids of Giza, their peaks pointing to the sky, still give rise to numerous questions. How were they built? Each pyramid consists of three thicknesses of stone blocks: those in the central core are built step fashion, with a second layer in the middle and then the outer layer, its stones smoothly fitted together without mortar.

Erecting these three levels, layer by layer, with virtually no technological aids is an extraordinary feat of engineering. How was it done? The most likely hypothesis is that the workers built one layer of stone at a time and piled around it a slightly sloping ramp of sand. As the building grew, the workers covered the sand ramps with tree trunks, which were used as rollers for sledges laden with the heavy stone slabs.

A RELIGION OF ETERNAL LIFE

When someone died, the family would carry the body to the sector where the embalmers lived and worked. There they would leave it for forty to seventy days, to go through the long process of mummification before burial. First the embalmers would remove the inner organs and place them in separate urns; then they would treat the body and organs in dry natron (a salt compound) to dry them out. The body was then laid on a huge alabaster table and wrapped in fine linen bandages, into which were inserted protective amulets provided by the family. The ritual embalmer then placed between the mummy's legs a papyrus roll. This roll, now called "The Book of the Dead," contained some good sayings about the deceased intended to help them in the next life. This kind of preparation was very expensive, and the poor could aspire to no more than a coarse woven wrapping with a few amulets, and burial in the desert sand.

Life after death was a major concern of the Egyptians, and it could only be guaranteed if the body was preserved as an imperishable container for the soul. Thus only the great were able to travel in Re's underground boat and accompany Osiris, god of vegetation and rebirth. Even then, those who desired eternal life had numerous obstacles to overcome. Demons, armed with knives, lay in wait for them. They had to pass through bolted doors and cross a mysterious labyrinth full of caverns. According to some traditions, a dead person who passed all these tests could enjoy eternal peace in the "Fields of Reeds," the paradise of the just. But the outcome of his journey depended on the judgment of Osiris, who weighed the heart, the seat of the soul, in the Hall of Double Justice. The name of the dead person was written on the coffin and the tomb as a symbol and guarantee of continued survival. For the Egyptians, giving something a name meant giving it life. To remove or mutilate someone's name brought eternal death. This is why people removed their enemies' names from monuments.

At birth, the name given to a child placed it under the protection of a particular god. Ptahmose meant "he who is born of Pteh"; Amenhotep meant "Ammon is satisfied"; Mutnedjmet meant "the goddess Mut is pleased." A name was thus a privilege, a link that united a person with the gods in life and at death became an indispensable guarantee of immortality.

This sarcophagus in painted wood bears the name of its owner, Hunamon; it dates from the Twenty-sixth Dynasty (663–525 B.C.) The designs and symbols are intended to protect the mummified body that rests inside for all time. The head is protected by the plumes of the vulture goddess Mut and the disk of the sun. Between the arms folded across the chest is a reference to the underground journey made by the dead person in the sacred boat of the sun god Re. A little below this stands the figure of Osiris, his face colored green as a reminder of the cycle of growth of vegetation and the renewal of life. Two goddesses, Isis and Nephthys, stretch their wings toward him in greeting. On the lower part of the coffin, the dead man is escorted by other divinities of the necropolis. There are even pictures of his burial place, the desert mountain, and the cow goddess Hathor. At his feet the wolf-headed god, Upuaut, opens up the way for him. (British Museum, London)

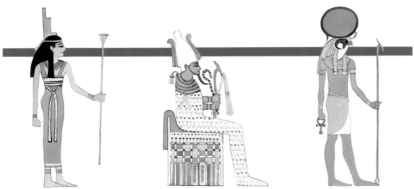

The Egyptians liked their gods to have families, usually consisting of three members. The best known is the family of Isis, her husband Osiris, and their son Horus. Osiris was killed by his brother Seth, who cut his body into pieces and threw them into the waters of the Nile. Isis roamed the earth in search of the scattered pieces and when she had found them put Osiris's body together again; the other gods allowed him to return to life.

Hathor, goddess of love and childbirth, wears the horns of a cow and the disk of the sun on her head.

Ptahmose, creator god, who came from Memphis.

Anubis, the jackal-faced guardian of the underworld.

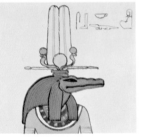

Sobek, the crocodile god from the marshes of Al Fayyūm.

Maat, wearing an ostrich feather, personified the balance of worldly order: truth and justice.

Mut, goddess wife of Ammon Re, wears a vulture skin and the royal crown.

Khnum, the ram-headed god, was "the Potter," who created human beings out of clay.

It was at a fairly late period, around the seventh century B.C., that the Egyptians began to worship certain animals, in the belief that they housed the spirits of the gods. This cat's mummy represents the goddess Bastet. The crocodile represented Sobek, god of Al Fayyūm, the bull Apis, and the ibis (a tall, slender bird), which was very often mummified, represented the god Thoth. (Louvre Museum)

Ammon, the god of Thebes, was portrayed as a man wearing a headdress of tall plumes. His name may have meant "the Hidden One." He carried several scepters, one of which was the ouas, symbol of stability. Originally a small local god, he became increasingly famed throughout the land during the Middle Kingdom, when the princes of Thebes rose to power.

This stele attests to the popularity of the cult of Osiris at Abydos. It was put up in memory of the royal herald Iamou-Nedjeh by his son. The donor is shown with his family close to the offering tables, which stand for the funeral rites necessary for the survival of the dead man. Rites would also be carried out by the college of funeral priests, the "servants of Ka," with whom the family had signed a contract. The hieroglyphic formulas reiterate the list of offerings made to the "Ka," the person's spirit double that lived on after death. At Abydos many other steles like this one have been found, inscribed with the prayers of the thousands of worshipers who made pilgrimages there between the sixteenth and twelfth centuries B.C.

27

DOCTORS AND MAGICIANS

When King Khufu grew bored at home in his palace, he would summon some of the most celebrated magicians to amuse him. The cleverest of all, it is told, was Djadjaemonkh, who could part the waters of the Nile and "fold" them in two, one half on top of the other. The magicians of Egypt were formidable; in the Bible we are told that when Moses came before them to persuade the pharaoh to let his people go, they turned their staffs into serpents and the river waters into blood!

All Egyptians made use of magicians and diviners. Magicians could protect them from everyday hazards, such as scorpion bites. Diviners provided them with love potions and amulets of good fortune, usually a jewel, which had a magical formula inserted or knotted within it. And to get the best results from medical treatment, it was common practice to combine it with magic. When medicines were prepared or taken, spells would be cast at the same time. A number of these practices have come down to us in papyrus texts. Some continued for a very long time; the Egyptians passed them on to the Greeks, who saw Isis as the great goddess of healing.

The doctors themselves had a good knowledge of the herbs that grew in Egypt and knew which were suitable for making unguents, drugs, and soothing poultices. There were a large number of recipes for eye lotions, for eye problems were prevalent around the Nile. The most common seems to have been blepharitis, a particularly painful inflammation of the eyelids. Some doctors specialized in surgery, and some could set broken bones. One papyrus describes various kinds of treatments performed during the New Kingdom, a period of warfare when many soldiers had serious wounds that needed attention. On the other hand, the Egyptians did not have a very good understanding of anatomy. Embalming procedures were so structured and ritualized that some parts of the body were never really studied or examined. Hence the Egyptians were quite ignorant about the functions of the bodily organs and not very good at treating illnesses caused by internal problems.

AMULETS

Amulets were worn as a protection; they were a kind of lucky charm, symbolizing the power of good forces over evil. One of them was the "Eye of Oudjat," or the eye of Horus, recalling the battle between Osiris and Seth. This was supposed to help a person triumph over his enemy. Then there was the Ouadj pillar, which helped a person keep his wealth, and the scarab (a beetle), sign of the rising sun and the continuation of life. The amulet shown here is in the form of the lion-headed dwarf-god Bes, who kept nightmares away from sleepers. (Louvre Museum)

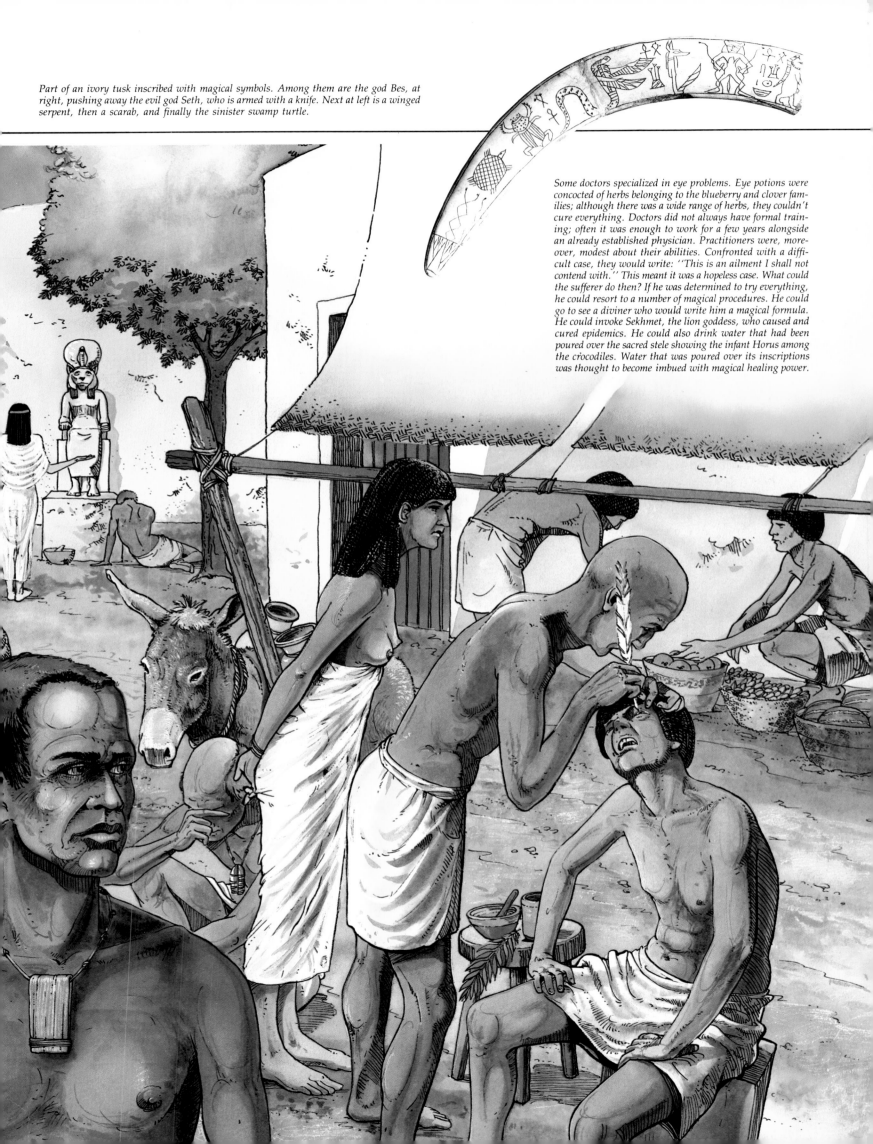

Part of an ivory tusk inscribed with magical symbols. Among them are the god Bes, at right, pushing away the evil god Seth, who is armed with a knife. Next at left is a winged serpent, then a scarab, and finally the sinister swamp turtle.

Some doctors specialized in eye problems. Eye potions were concocted of herbs belonging to the blueberry and clover families; although there was a wide range of herbs, they couldn't cure everything. Doctors did not always have formal training; often it was enough to work for a few years alongside an already established physician. Practitioners were, moreover, modest about their abilities. Confronted with a difficult case, they would write: ''This is an ailment I shall not contend with.'' This meant it was a hopeless case. What could the sufferer do then? If he was determined to try everything, he could resort to a number of magical procedures. He could go to see a diviner who would write him a magical formula. He could invoke Sekhmet, the lion goddess, who caused and cured epidemics. He could also drink water that had been poured over the sacred stele showing the infant Horus among the crocodiles. Water that was poured over its inscriptions was thought to become imbued with magical healing power.

LIFE IN
THE NILE VALLEY

As evening drew near, the houses by the river banks would still be warm from the heat of the sun. Children would come out to play in the cool shade; some of them had little jointed wooden crocodiles that they could draw along, the older ones played checkers, and the sports-loving played ball games. It is clear from many paintings that the Egyptians had great respect for family life; marriages were always monogamous, with the exception of the pharaoh, who maintained a regular harem.

Every family had its own house. Houses had only a single story and were often built adjoining each other. They had flat roofs, which were used as terraces; people slept out on them during the suffocatingly hot nights of summer. In the central room smoke from a fire rose up through a hole in the roof, which served as a chimney. In the evening the glowing embers and a few oil lamps shed a dim light as the housewife prepared the evening meal.

The basic food was bread. With it were served vegetables, salads, beans, and onions, which everyone grew in gardens within the village. The most common drink was beer, made with fermented barley. Children drank goats' milk or a little cow's milk. The consumption of meat was low; it was very expensive, and was reserved for the feasts of kings and important dignitaries.

Different types of oil were used for cooking, for burning in lamps, and above all for preparing unguents and perfumes, which were popular at all levels of society. At festival times, women would wear a linen cone on their heads filled with a perfumed unguent, which would slowly melt into their hair.

All the pottery containers for perfumes, provisions, and drinks were made in the village itself; so also was wine, which was carefully corked, dated, labeled, and stored. The people were experts at weaving. Baskets, bags, sandals, and mats were woven by the hundreds out of different types of rush growing in the district. The land remained largely rural, and daily life continued for three thousand years with very little change. The pace of provincial life was slow in this country where people only traveled in the service of the king.

The Egyptians were very fond of their children and made a great fuss over them. They are often referred to in their writings and shown in their paintings. Very small children had their heads shaved, except for a plait, or braid, on one side. There is a statue of King Ramses as a child with his hair like this, sucking his finger, maybe to help him go to sleep.

THE SERPENT GAME

An alabaster game board in the form of a serpent coiled in a spiral. Players used colored balls and figurines of lions or dogs. Neither the rules of the game nor its meaning are known, but some people believe it may have been an ancestor of Snakes and Ladders. (Louvre Museum)

Daily life beside the great river.

In the foreground, the house of a well-to-do civil servant stands on the outskirts of town close to the river. It is larger than the other houses and surrounded by a huge garden, which contains an orchard with some vine trellises, a small kitchen garden, and a pleasure garden. In the pleasure garden is a water-lily pool and a small summer house where the family can go to relax during the heat of the day.

In the late afternoon the family sits under an awning, listening to musicians, while a servant carries jugs to the house in preparation for the evening meal. The house may not seem very large by our standards, but the Egyptians spent much of their lives outdoors. To keep out the heat, there are only a few small windows. The next-door neighbors are relaxing on their terrace roof.

THE END
OF A CIVILIZATION

The reign of Ramses II saw Egypt at its full flowering. After that, beginning in 1100 B.C., came a period of troubles and decline. There was a series of weak pharaohs whose power deteriorated, and the country fell into anarchy and confusion. For nearly three centuries, competing dynasties tried to squeeze what they could out of the decaying empire.

Egypt was a tempting prey to foreign powers. In the seventh century B.C. the fierce Assyrian warriors "came down like the wolf on the fold," ravaging Syria and arriving at the edge of the Nile. The Assyrian conquest began in 675 B.C. and ended with King Ashurbanipal's great expedition in 666, when the whole country was occupied as far as Thebes. Shortly afterward Egypt recovered, under the leadership of Psamtik I (663–610 B.C.), who managed to drive out the invaders with the help of foreign mercenaries. With the next pharaoh, Psamtik's son Necho II (610–594 B.C.), there was even a return to prosperity. To improve trade, Necho began digging a canal linking the Nile to the Red Sea, and tried to recover Egypt's territories in Asia; but here he came up against Nebuchadrezzar, the powerful king of Babylon, who defeated him decisively at the Battle of Carçhemish in 605 B.C.

Now exhausted after centuries of glory, Egypt passed from hand to hand, from one conqueror to the next. In 529 B.C. Egypt fell into the hands of Persia, whose king, Darius, incorporated it into his growing empire and ordered the completion of the canal begun by Necho. Egypt rebelled several times, and as a result the yoke of the occupier became ever more tyrannical. When Alexander the Great arrived in 332 B.C. he was hailed as a liberator. He entrusted Egypt to one of his generals, Ptolemy, who founded the Ptolemaic Dynasty. Under these Greek princes Egypt returned to a long period of peace and economic prosperity. In the third century B.C. it was the greatest maritime and commercial power in the Near East.

But on the horizon of the first century B.C. loomed the threat of a new master—Rome. Cleopatra, the last of the Ptolemies, did all she could to save Egypt from the humiliation of annexation. She allied herself to Anthony, the Roman general (imperator) who ruled the eastern Mediterranean. This, however, did not suit the plans of Octavius (Augustus), the general who controlled the western Mediterranean. In 31 B.C. he beat Anthony and Cleopatra's army at Actium, on the west coast of Greece. Egypt became a Roman province—a province with a difference, however. It still carried enormous prestige and, very importantly, it was the richest. The Roman emperors were careful about which of their generals they sent there, in case any more should be seduced into rebellion.

Egyptian culture, religion, and architecture fascinated the Roman conquerors. For example, the citizen Gaius Cestius had his tomb built in Rome in the shape of a pyramid. The cult of Isis reached the heart of the capital: Isis became the great healer of the Romans and also, as the Stella Maris (the "Star of the Sea), the protectress of sailors. The religion of the pharaohs looked as if it would last forever. However, in 395 A.D. it received its death blow from Christianity, when the emperor Theodosius closed down all the pagan temples. This was the point at which Egyptian civilization truly died.

In 332 B.C. the great conqueror Alexander entered Egypt without much opposition; the people were weary of oppression under Persian domination. Religion and the priesthood still had a very strong influence. After taking possession of the Delta and the north, he went to the Oasis of Ammon, which had long been the shrine of a famous oracle. In those days everyone, from the most ordinary private citizen to the most powerful king, questioned the oracles. We may wonder whether Alexander, about to conduct a campaign in Asia, did the same. It seems likely that he did. It is known that he was received by a delegation of Egyptian priests and, leaving his army outside the holy precincts, he went into the sanctuary alone. But he never told anyone what had been revealed to him. Shortly afterward, he left Egypt; however, he left traces of his occupation, including the founding of the city of Alexandria, in the north of the Delta.

This bas-relief from the Temple of Esna was carved in Roman times and shows a Roman emperor in the costume of a pharaoh. The Emperors who lived in Rome, such as Trajan and Hadrian, were regarded by the Egyptians as continuing in the dynastic line of the pharaohs. The emperor is therefore shown as a high priest in the temple of the gods. Much later, after the "pagan" cults had been abolished, the Temple of Esna was used as a church by the first Christians in Egypt, the Copts. You can see the cross they carved, just behind the figure of the king.

THE HITTITE EMPIRE

At the end of the third millennium B.C. a new people crossed the mountain chains of the Caucasus and entered Anatolia. With them they brought a new animal, the horse, which they were among the first peoples to domesticate. They used it both for riding and for drawing their powerful chariots, which were much feared in battle. Equally formidable were their lethal iron weapons, fashioned by smiths whose metalworking skills were superior to all.

The clay tablets of the Assyrian merchants of the day called them "Hatti" or "Hittites." In wave after wave they settled on the Anatolian plain. They founded small principalities that shared the same customs and beliefs, and by the eighteenth century B.C. they had created the beginnings of an empire. Around 1650 the Hittites built themselves a fortified capital at Hattushash, now Bogazköv, in Turkey.

Anatolia was an arid, inhospitable country, searingly hot in summer, swept by icy winds in winter. The Hittites began turning their thoughts to the rich lands of the south—Syria and Babylonia—with their great rivers and lush green oases. They began by making looting skirmishes, which developed into full-scale battles. In 1595 the Hittites took Babylon. But it was not until two centuries later, in the reign of Shuppiluliumash (1380–1336 B.C.), that they became the greatest power in the Near East. The new empire extended from the Caucasus to the Orontes River, from the Euphrates to the eastern Mediterranean, where it threatened the great power of neighboring Egypt by cutting off some of its Syrian allies.

But the glory of the Hittites did not last long. After the death of Shuppiluliumash, the empire was weakened by sedition and internal rivalries, and fell prey to the ambitions of its neighbors. It fell beneath the warlike might of Assyria, which seized its southern territories. The final blow was dealt by the Achaeans, new invaders from the north of Greece, in the twelfth century B.C. The Hittites left the field to the new powers and fell into obscurity. Here and there some carvings and stone lions recall the splendor of a vanished empire.

The supreme god of the Hittite pantheon was Teshub, god of the storm, "king of the sky, sovereign of the land of the Hatti." His emblems were the double ax and a streak of lightning. His consort was the sun goddess Arinna, who was also highly revered. In addition, the Hittites worshiped nearly 2,000 other deities! They had adopted some of them from the ancient peoples of Anatolia, as well as their neighbors, the Hurrians. Of course, they needed a vast number of temples and priests to serve all these gods. Their places of worship were in the open air, like the rocky shrine of Yazilikaya. (Ankara Museum)

THE ART OF METALWORKING

The Hittites' great wealth was founded on the rich supply of mineral ore in Anatolia. They used iron to make tools and weapons and were partially responsible for spreading its use throughout the Near East. But they were master bronzesmiths and delighted in making beautiful ornaments like this one in the form of a stag. This piece, which was used to decorate the top of a flagpole, dates from the end of the third millennium B.C.. (Ankara Museum)

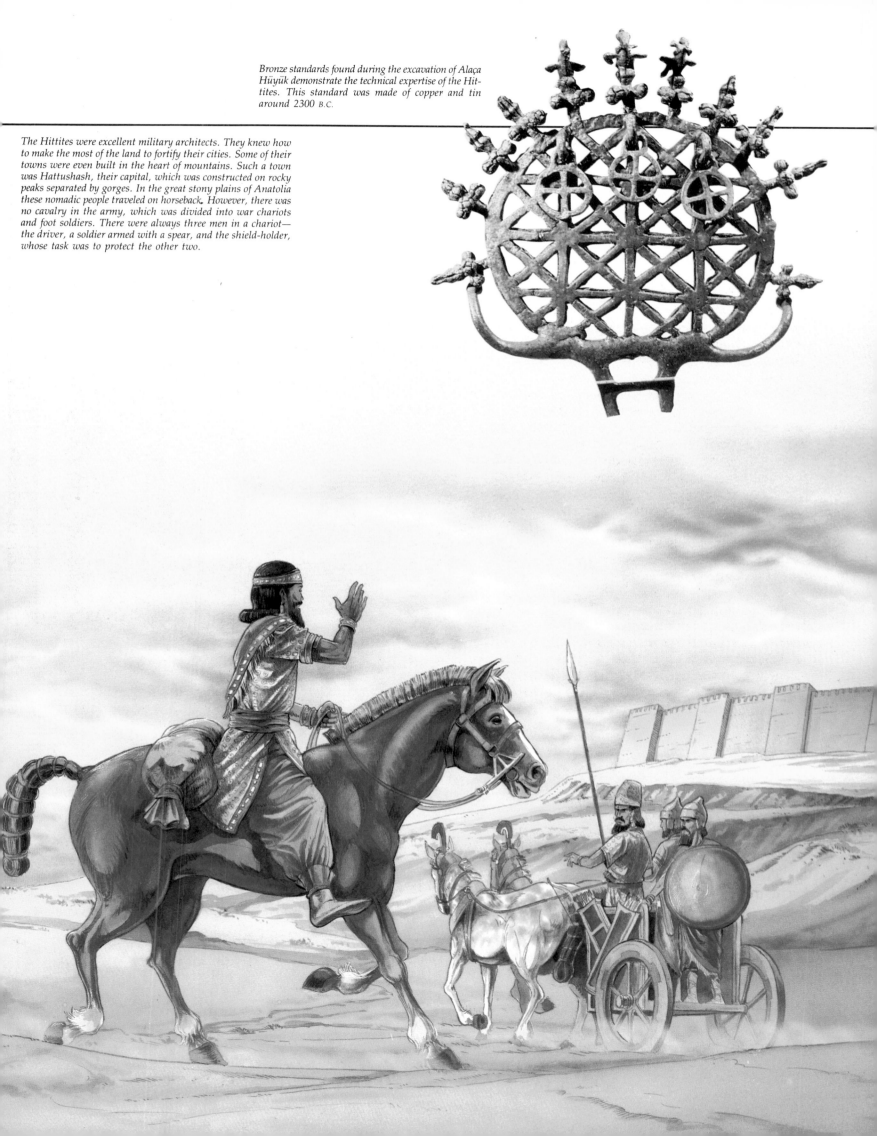

Bronze standards found during the excavation of Alaça Hüyük demonstrate the technical expertise of the Hittites. This standard was made of copper and tin around 2300 B.C.

The Hittites were excellent military architects. They knew how to make the most of the land to fortify their cities. Some of their towns were even built in the heart of mountains. Such a town was Hattushash, their capital, which was constructed on rocky peaks separated by gorges. In the great stony plains of Anatolia these nomadic people traveled on horseback. However, there was no cavalry in the army, which was divided into war chariots and foot soldiers. There were always three men in a chariot—the driver, a soldier armed with a spear, and the shield-holder, whose task was to protect the other two.

THE ASSYRIANS

For a very long time the Assyrians had occupied the upper Tigris Valley in Mesopotamia, where they had settled as peaceful farmers and cattle raisers. At the end of the third millennium B.C., their busy merchants had set up flourishing businesses in neighboring Anatolia. But they were also warriors—conquerors waiting for their hour to come—and when it did, they would be renowned for their cruelty to those they conquered.

In the third century B.C. they erupted brutally into the Near East, making surprise attacks, burning and massacring everything and everyone in their way. In the south, they swallowed up the remnants of the crumbling Hittite Empire. These were no simple bandits. They had a remarkably well-equipped army, the trump card in their campaign of conquest.

Their main force was the cavalry, along with the war chariots that protected the movements of the troops. They enlarged their infantry, which was divided into spearsmen on one side and archers and slingsmen, with their lighter weapons, on the other. In addition, they had excellent military engineers armed with battering rams and huge siege engines, and reliable support services that included maintenance men, storekeepers and servants, and a particularly efficient network of spies. Led by dynamic rulers experienced in warfare, this army enabled the Assyrians in the seventh century B.C. to win the greatest empire up to that time, stretching from the Persian Gulf in the east to Cyprus in the west, from Armenia in the north to Arabia in the south.

It was the king's duty, as high priest and estate manager of the god Ashur, to enlarge the supreme god's territory; this was his justification for waging a kind of "holy war" against all the neighboring peoples. The empire was not interested in assimilating the peoples it conquered. Its chief purpose was to exploit its conquests for the sole benefit of Nineveh, the capital city. With the help of an efficiently run administration, it imposed tributes, military service, and forced labor to work on its great buildings. The machinery of repression ground relentlessly on, allowing no respite or relief. Every spring the army would march out to crush rebel uprisings; as soon as they left, new revolts would break out in the conquered regions. The strongest resistance came from Babylon, which waged a continuous war of attrition and finally shook the power of Assyria.

Fierce and war-loving though they were, the Assyrians were also gifted artists, and have left us some very fine bas-reliefs, though mainly inspired by hunting and warfare. The great king Ashurbanipal (688–627 B.C.) was a lover of literature and at Nineveh he built an enormous library, where several thousand tablets captured from vanquished nations were stored with great care. It is paradoxical that the Assyrians, who destroyed so much, have made it possible for us to know the great literary texts of the Sumerians, an early race in Mesopotamia.

The Assyrians were feared and hated by all, and their downfall was greeted with general relief. This came about when Kyaxares, king of Media, formed an alliance with the Babylonian king Nabopolassar. In 626 B.C. they set out to destroy Assyria and, despite ferocious resistance, they succeeded. Assyria fell in 609 B.C.

The Assyrians were great builders. Everything had to be on a colossal scale, starting with the kings' palaces. The palace of Sargon II at Khorsabad covers about 25 acres and contains 209 rooms and courtyards. To guard the entrance, the king commissioned his sculptors to create enormous human-headed winged bulls, and personally supervised their transport. Just one of these giant statues weighs between 12 and 14 tons and is over 12 feet long. The statue shown here has been hoisted onto a kind of sledge and is being hauled along by four lines of prisoners. Other prisoners are putting down wooden rollers to help move it along. And still others are using levers to lift the back end of the statue.

BY FIRE AND THE SWORD

From the Tigris to the Euphrates, from Syria to the Zagros Mountains, the conquerors left behind a trail of terror, fire, and pillage. The Assyrians and the Babylonians alike brought down the scourge of war on the backs of nations that lived in perpetual terror of sieges and massacres. Little had changed since the times of the first cities—Ur, Lagash, and Mari.

Every year, "by command of Ashur," the Assyrian king would lead his chariots and foot soldiers over the dusty trails. He would harass the enemy and finally force them into submission by laying siege to their principal fortress, which protected both people and possessions. The king killed, looted, and burned all before him to make sure that there was no possible revival of resistance once he had passed by. Speaking of one of these "expeditions," the Assyrian king Ashurbanipal wrote in his *Annals*: "I built a pillar before the gate of the city and I flayed all the chiefs who had rebelled against me and stretched their skin on the pillar . . . Some I impaled on stakes . . . I burned many of the prisoners amongst them . . . I cut off the arms or hands of some . . . I plucked out their eyes . . . I laid low six thousand five hundred of their warriors with the sword and the survivors perished of thirst in the desert."

But when he needed a work force, the king took large numbers of prisoners home with him. The practice of deportation was born; in fact, it had probably started with the Sumerians. After a town had been besieged, long lines of captives—including women and children—would take the road of exile, escorted and closely guarded by soldiers. Entire populations were moved in this fashion, as far as possible from their native lands, which would make them less likely to rebel. Sargon II, king of Assyria from 721 to 705 B.C., boasted of having deported 27,290 prisoners from the town of Samaria in Palestine; his son Sennacherib spoke of deporting 200,150 natives of the kingdom of Judah and later the Babylonian king Nebuchadrezzar included among his glorious deeds the removal of 8,000 Jews after the capture of Jerusalem in 586 B.C.

Large numbers of these captives died on the journey through lack of food, water, and care. Those who reached the land of exile were very quickly put to work on the great building projects, or in the fields or the temple workrooms. Most craftsmen were allowed to practice their trade. The most highly valued were metalworkers, who could be relied on to make good weapons. Among the 8,000 Jews deported from Jerusalem, Nebuchadrezzar took care to include a selection of a thousand iron forgers and metalworkers. Weavers, goldsmiths, and joiners were also prized in the kingdom of Babylon, where the nobility had a taste for embroidery, jewels, and fine furniture. The lot of the deportees may not have been as tragic as it has been described by the prophets of Israel. They had been brought there to play an important role in the economy, and their social status was higher than that of slaves. When Cyrus of Persia liberated the Jews from Babylon in 538 B.C., some of them had become integrated into local life, and chose to stay where they were.

Woe to the defeated! The fate of those who escaped massacre was exile. This Assyrian bas-relief from the seventh century B.C. depicts women and children led by soldiers; it gave visitors to the palace of Nineveh something to think about. (Louvre Museum)

"I struck down six thousand five hundred of their warriors with the sword and the survivors perished of thirst in the desert."

The final stage of a military campaign was the siege of the enemy's towns. Like the Babylonians, the Assyrians were extremely well equipped. They dug ditches and put up ladders against the ramparts; they made wooden siege-towers on wheels, dug tunnels under the ramparts, and bombarded the towers and walls with catapults, finishing off the work of destruction with pickaxes. When a town was captured, it was systematically sacked. Few of the great cities escaped during this time. Thebes, Samaria, Jerusalem, Nineveh, and the prestigious city of Babylon were all devastated in their turn, sometimes more than once.

THE GLORY OF BABYLON

Today practically nothing remains of Babylon ("gate of god"), possibly the most famous city of antiquity, and the inspiration for the biblical Babel. But the people who visited it in its days of splendor were duly impressed. The prophet Isaiah called it, "The glory of kingdoms, the beauty of the Chaldees' excellency." And Jeremiah, who predicted its downfall, described it this way: "A wine cup at the hand of Jehovah, making the whole earth mad." No less lyrical was Herodotus, the famous Greek historian and traveler, who described it as the most powerful city of the Near East since the fall of Nineveh, in 612 B.C.

When the Assyrian Empire crumbled, the Babylonians were sole masters of Mesopotamia. On the still smoking ruins of the Assyrian palaces, Nabopolassar (reigned 625–605 B.C.), founder of the Chaldean Dynasty, took only two decades to rebuild a vast empire between the Tigris and the Euphrates. With his son Nebuchadrezzar II (reigned 604–562 B.C.) Babylon recovered the prestige it had known under the great king Hammurabi in the eighteenth century B.C.

Babylon was the jewel in the crown of this brilliant civilization. Already nearly two thousand years old, the city had almost disappeared completely in 689 B.C., when the Assyrian king Sennacherib had tried to turn it into a swamp by diverting the waters of the Euphrates so that they would wear away the mud brick walls and literally bring the city down. The Chaldean kings rebuilt, enlarged, and fortified Babylon, adding to its splendors with monuments and fine buildings. At an unbelievable cost in money and labor, it was surrounded by a double wall reinforced with towers, protected by moats or trenches, and pierced with eight monumental gates, each named after a god or goddess.

Over 100,000 people lived in Babylon in the sixth century B.C. Built on the edge of a beautiful oasis, the city stretched over both banks of the Euphrates. From miles away could be seen the huge seven-story ziggurat, nearly 300 feet high, which dominated the city. It was called Etemenanki, "the house of the foundation of the sky and the earth." It was dedicated to Marduk, guardian god of Babylon, as were many other of the city's temples. In all, it is said that there were over a thousand places of worship in Babylon. The Gate of Ishtar, magnificently ornamented in blue enamel, was famous throughout the ancient world, and the Hanging Gardens of Nebuchadrezzar's palace were one of the Seven Wonders of the World. The gardens, which grew on stepped terraces, were planted with palms, ferns, climbing plants, and thousands of flowers. A machine worked by laborers lifted water up from the river to refresh the precious plants.

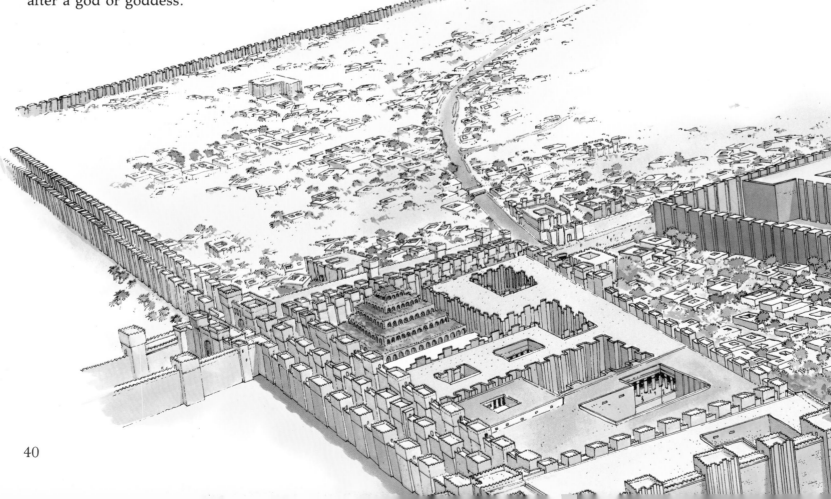

"The glory of kingdoms, the beauty of the Chaldees' excellency,"
"A wine cup at the hand of Jehovah . . ."

Between the Gate of Ishtar and the Temple of Marduk ran the Processional Way, the sacred highway of Babylon. It was 65 feet wide and paved in white stones. On either side of it ran two tall enameled walls, decorated with 6-foot- high lions in molded and varnished brick, symbols of the goddess Ishtar. They were shown roaring to frighten away evil spirits. (Louvre Museum)

MARDUK IN HIS CITY

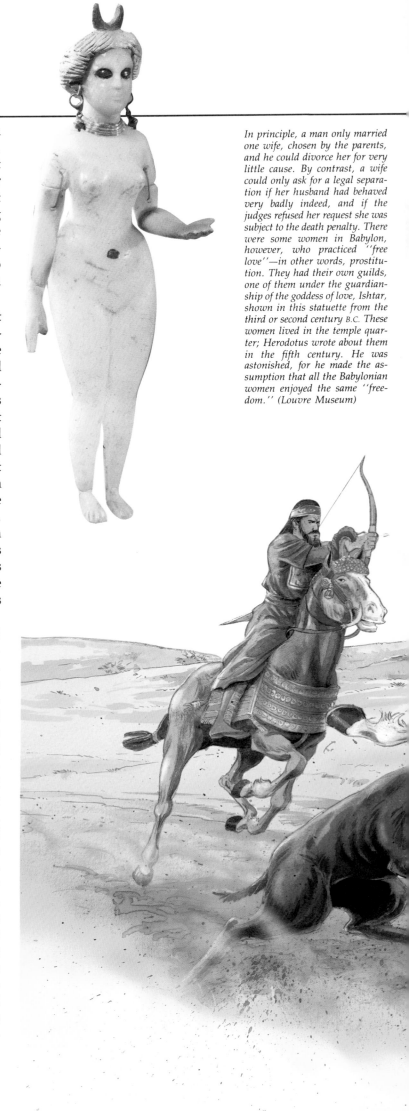

Every year with the arrival of spring, daily life in Babylon came to a halt. From the great king to the lowliest slave, everyone forgot everything except the most important feast day on the calendar, the New Year Festival. The New Year was celebrated around the time of the spring equinox, and it was primarily a fertility cult. When nature awoke after the long winter, the Babylonians remembered what they owed to the produce of the soil. But the new year also signified the reestablishment of the order of the world. And it was important to ensure the goodwill of Marduk, chief god of the Babylonian religion.

The ceremonies went on for eleven days, mainly at Marduk's great temple, the Esagila. On the fifth day a specially appointed priest, the mashmashu, sprinkled the walls of the temple with holy water, to purify them. A butcher would decapitate a sheep, whose body was carried through the temple and then thrown into the Euphrates. The dead body was believed to take with it all the signs of the previous year. That evening, a strange ceremony would take place. The king would come to the Esagila for the first time during the festival and hand over his scepter and crown to the high priest. The priest would accept them, then pull the king's ears and make him bow at the foot of Marduk's statue; there he would force the king to confess his sins and ask the god's forgiveness for them. On the ninth day, the king would lead a procession through the town of a dozen chariots carrying statues of all the gods and goddesses. A great feast was held, accompanied by hymns and prayers. On the eleventh day everyone went home, the gods to their temples, the king to his palace. The festival was over, and Babylon's future assured for the year to come.

Babylonian society may have been united during festival times, but it was built on a hierarchical system. The great temples owned the finest estates, accumulated the most wealth, and controlled economic life. Most of the town craftsmen were employed by them. They tended to gather in particular quarters, according to their trade, and they formed well-organized guilds. Trades were passed down through families from one generation to the next, although sometimes slaves were allowed in as apprentices. Slavery was a common condition in Babylon. Prisoners of war were slaves, as were citizens who could not pay their debts, and children were sold into slavery by poor families. Slaves were indispensable to the national economy.

The Babylonian penal code descended from the Code of Hammurabi, and it reflected the social inequalities. If someone committed an act of violence against a person of the same social class, they were punished with a simple fine. But if they were to perpetrate the same crime on someone of superior rank, a severe corporal punishment was imposed. Many punishments were retaliatory: someone who attacked a pregnant woman was punished by having his own child killed; an architect whose building fell down had his own house pulled down, and if a death had been caused, one of his children would be executed. Of course, it is not known for certain whether the full strength of the law was actually applied in such cases. It seems very likely that aside from the most serious crimes, these severe punishments were replaced by fines.

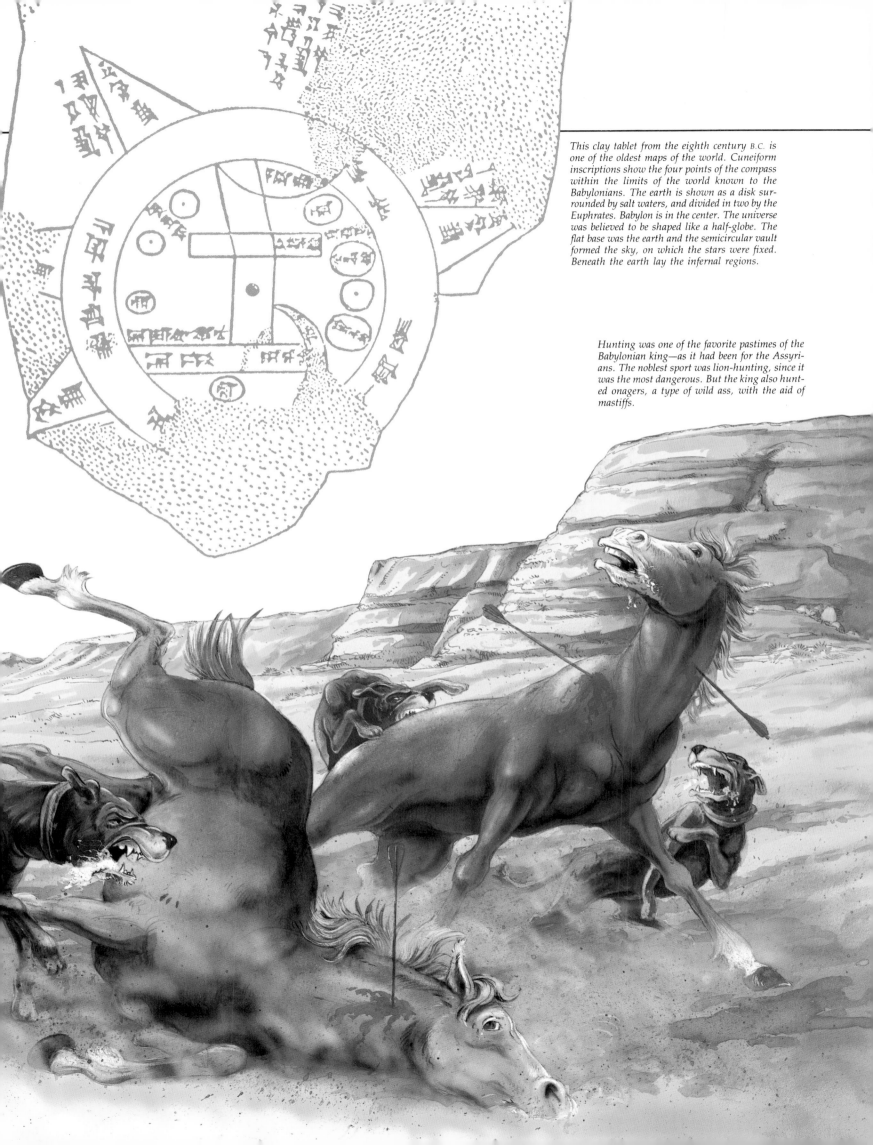

This clay tablet from the eighth century B.C. is one of the oldest maps of the world. Cuneiform inscriptions show the four points of the compass within the limits of the world known to the Babylonians. The earth is shown as a disk surrounded by salt waters, and divided in two by the Euphrates. Babylon is in the center. The universe was believed to be shaped like a half-globe. The flat base was the earth and the semicircular vault formed the sky, on which the stars were fixed. Beneath the earth lay the infernal regions.

Hunting was one of the favorite pastimes of the Babylonian king—as it had been for the Assyrians. The noblest sport was lion-hunting, since it was the most dangerous. But the king also hunted onagers, a type of wild ass, with the aid of mastiffs.

DIPLOMATS
AND MERCHANTS

There exists a letter written in displeasure by Amenophis IV to Aziru, a Syrian prince, accusing him of disloyalty to the Egyptian alliance. Aziru had just taken part in the sacking of a neighboring city, in collaboration with Egypt's enemies, the Hittites. But he vehemently defended himself; he sent the pharaoh valuable gifts in appeasement, and confirmed that he would receive his ambassador, "in submission."

When kings were not busy making war, they devoted much of their energy to developing good relations with each other. They swore mutual friendship and respect, and sent each other ambassadors, letters, and splendid presents. These royal missions were accompanied by trading caravans, which welcomed the protection of army officers. Sometimes, the envoys themselves carried merchandise destined to be sold in foreign markets. The roles of merchant and diplomat were often combined.

Constant warfare, far from hampering the economic development of the Near East, helped it by opening up great international highways for the transport of manufactured goods and raw materials. Towns were the first to benefit from the growing movement of commerce. The most brilliant and heavily populated was without doubt Tyre. It was ideally located on the Mediterranean coast at the point where goods had to pass through from Egypt and Mesopotamia. Here there was a constant traffic of copper, wood, linen, wool, alum, gold, ivory, glassware, and papyrus, not to mention wine, cereals, and oil.

Merchants' caravans and royal ambassadors
traveled the highways of the Middle East.

*Merchants labeled their merchandise with their own
seals, which they stamped into soft clay. Seals often
depicted the deities that protected their trades. This
blue seal, showing a man at prayer, comes from Babylon. (Louvre Museum)*

*Merchants gathering on the outskirts of a town. Some
of them have traveled very long distances in carts
drawn by donkeys or oxen. In the twelfth century
B.C. merchants began using camels, and long
caravans began to tread the trails to Arabia with its
perfumed resins and to India with its precious spices.
A lot of bargaining took place in the market. Fabrics,
pottery, and wood exchanged hands; so did iron
which, between the tenth and eighth centuries B.C.,
steadily replaced bronze for making weapons and
everyday items. Money was not widely used as a
medium of exchange; it only appeared with the Persians in the sixth century. However, coins like the
gold mina and talents of silver, copper, or tin were
used for accounting purposes during business trans-
actions. Scribes were always around to record and control the accounts, and this enabled the government
to levy taxes. An old Sumerian proverb declared:
"You can have a master, you can have a king, but
the man to fear is the tax collector!"*

THE PERSIANS

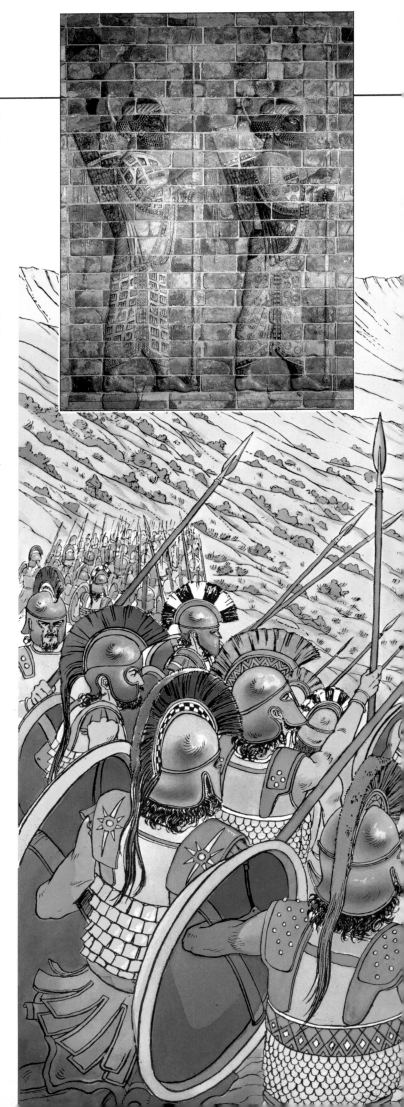

Swept by the cold winds of winter, heavy with dust and heat in summer, the Iranian Plateau was crossed during several centuries by numerous bands of horsemen. These warlike nomads progressed from east to west, hoping to leave behind the inhospitable steppes and plains to settle in their turn in the fertile crescent of Mesopotamia. They were waiting for the first, slightest chink in the armor of the neighboring empires. In the seventh century B.C., when Ashurbanipal ruled Assyria, they gained territory toward the west and began striking terror around them.

The Medes, inhabitants of the kingdom of Media and allies of the Babylonian king Nabopolassar, made continual attacks, which led to the final fall of the Assyrian Empire in 609 B.C. However, it was the Persian ruler Cyrus who, 59 years later, was to unite the Medes and the Persians under his rule, paving the way for the establishment of a great new empire. In less than twenty years he conquered the entire area from the Indus River in the east to the Tigris and Euphrates valley in the west, including the Greek cities on the Aegean coast.

Cyrus was clever; he was able to combine his greed for conquest with a generous attitude toward the countries and peoples he conquered. In 539 B.C. he seized Babylon with almost no resistance and allowed the Jews exiled there by Nebuchadrezzar to return to Palestine. At his death, in 529, all that was left standing against the Persian Empire and the ruling dynasty (the Achaemenid Dynasty) was a single great state that had dominated the history of the Near East for nearly two thousand years—Egypt. And Egypt was conquered by Cyrus's son Cambyses in 525 B.C.

Keeping together a vast conglomeration of peoples as varied as the Medes, Babylonians, Syrians, Phoenicians, Lydians, Ionian Greeks, Egyptians, and Aryans, from Persia to the Indus, was no small undertaking. Darius I (reigned 522–486 B.C.) succeeded in organizing the empire by introducing a flexible system of government. He divided it into twenty provinces, each called a satrapy, each ruled by a governor who was allowed a certain degree of autonomy in maintaining public order. This system enabled him to bring in regular annual taxes, in proportion to the wealth of each satrapy and the size of the military contingent recruited from it. Darius took the precaution of having his satrapies overseen by a civil servant and financial adviser, as well as a military commander. Each saw to it that the others remained loyal and obedient.

Aramaic became the official language for the administration of the whole empire. It was spoken alongside all the different languages of the subject peoples. The army also served as a unifying element. It consisted of a corps recruited from all the satrapies. Their activities were supervised by a vigilant royal guard, made up of 15,000 able soldiers, a mixture of Medes and Persians. Persian rule introduced a new unity to the administration of its whole empire; it spread the use of money, which the Lydians had invented; it brought in a unified system of weights and measures based on the Babylonian standard; and finally, it encouraged the development and maintenance of a vast network of roads used by the royal horsemen.

The archers formed the elite of the Persian
army. The enemy would retreat before the
showers of arrows from their bows. In this
frieze from the palace of Susa (around 520
B.C.) archers are shown wearing costumes
decorated with braids and embroidery. They
are armed with lances and carry bows and
sheaths of arrows on their backs.

In 499 B.C. an uprising by the Greek villages of Ionia led to Darius's first expedition and the destruction of Miletus in 494. But the Athenians encouraged the Ionians to resist. Darius, determined to put a stop to Athens, landed in the Bay of
Marathon in September 490, with nearly 30,000 horsemen. Despite their obvious
superiority, the Persians were repulsed by 10,000 hoplites (heavily armed foot soldiers) led by the Athenian general Miltiades, and forced to re-embark quickly. Darius
had been irritated on a previous occasion by the arrogance of the Greeks, and had
ordered one of his servants to repeat to him three times a day, "Master, remember
the Athenians!" After this disastrous battle he was not likely to forget them.

THE KING
OF KINGS

In the vast hall of the palace at Persepolis, the great king, impassive, received gifts brought by messengers from the twenty-eight kingdoms of the empire. The Medean envoy, staff in hand, advanced and bowed to the throne, closely watched by the imperial dignitaries. The faithful members of the royal guard were there, too, ready to pounce at the slightest provocation. But Darius wanted the Festival of the Tribute to take place in peace. Was he not the king of all his subjects? "I am Darius, the Great King, King of Kings, King of the Countries, King of the Earth, the son of Hystaspes of Achaemenia," he proclaimed in the charter of foundation of his palace at Susa.

He had not had an easy time gaining the throne. In 522 B.C. the reign of Cambyses ended when the power was usurped by the Magus Gaumata (the Magi were a priestly sect). The story goes that after eliminating Gaumata, Darius was chosen as king by geomancy, a type of divination that chose as winner the person whose horse neighed first at dawn. Gossips also said that his squire resorted to cheating to make sure his horse was the first to neigh. The opening years of his reign were tumultuous, entirely devoted to putting down the rebellions that broke out almost everywhere as a result of the battle for succession. Once these were settled, Darius threw himself into a massive building program. To Pasargadae, the capital founded by Cyrus in 559 B.C., he added two new imperial cities: Susa—the ancient capital of Elam, which the Assyrians had destroyed and which he rebuilt, and Persepolis, which he made his capital.

All the kingdoms contributed to the building of Persepolis. The palace at Susa included wood from Lebanon and Gandhara (now western Pakistan), gold from Sardis (capital of the kingdom of Lydia) and Bactria (in the north of Afghanistan), silver and ebony from Egypt, and ivory from Ethiopia and India. The craftsmen, too, came from all over the empire: the stonecutters were Ionians, the goldsmiths Egyptians and Medes, the joiners Babylonians. This combination of influences made Persian art into a bold synthesis of all the artistic elements of the East. Darius and his successors liked to have their walls decorated with molded enameled bricks from Babylon, and lions, griffons (a breed of dog), and archers marched along the walls of Susa. They also decorated their palaces with hundreds of bas-reliefs, in imitation of the Assyrians. Unlike Assyrian carvings, however, these never depicted warfare. The Achaemenid kings forbade any representation of the warlike deeds that had brought them to power, preferring instead to present an idealistic vision of a pacified empire, as can be seen in the reliefs of tribute bearers in the Apadana (audience hall) of Persepolis. Where the Assyrians had aimed to express their power and inspire fear, the Persians showed themselves to be more tactful, and avoided humiliating those they conquered.

In 512 B.C. Darius, still drunk with conquest, invaded Thrace and began a series of wars that his opponents, the Greeks, spoke of as the "Medean Wars." For the first time, the East found itself in direct contact with another civilization. Receptive to foreign influences, the Persian Empire learned about the culture and values of Greece, unknowingly preparing itself for the arrival of its great conqueror, Alexander.

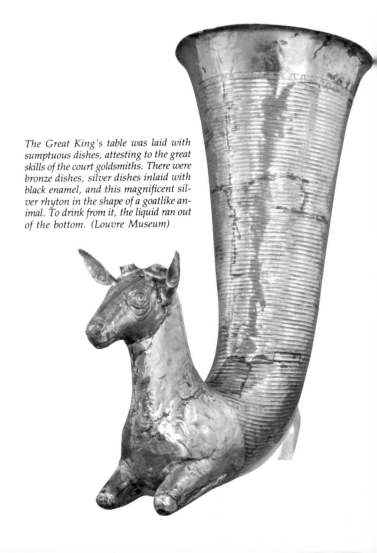

The Great King's table was laid with sumptuous dishes, attesting to the great skills of the court goldsmiths. There were bronze dishes, silver dishes inlaid with black enamel, and this magnificent silver rhyton in the shape of a goatlike animal. To drink from it, the liquid ran out of the bottom. (Louvre Museum)

48

Near the modern town of Shīrāz, in southwestern Iran, lie the remains of Darius's city, Persepolis. It was begun in 520 B.C. and its building was continued until 460 by the Great King's successors, Xerxes and Artaxerxes I. Set in a magnificent landscape with the mountains in the distance, the immense Apadana of the kings was actually made up of several palaces; each king had his own. The audience hall of Darius's palace was 150 feet square and was said to hold 10,000 people. Persepolis was captured and partly destroyed by Alexander the Great in 331 B.C. In the Middle Ages its impressive ruins attracted many travelers. But it was not until 1931 that excavations were started that would reveal the full splendor of this great city.

"I love justice," Darius declared, "and have never loved lies." The preoccupation with justice expressed by this Persian sovereign had its roots in the official Persian religion, Mazdaism. It was founded around 600 B.C. by Zoroaster, a priest and religious reformer, whom the Greeks called Zarathustra. Taking some of its sources from the ancient Indo-European beliefs in a number of gods, Zoroaster turned it into a monotheistic religion, with Ahura Mazda as the supreme god, creator of the world. Ahura Mazda governed abstract ideas such as Justice and Deceit; he left mankind free to choose between one or the other, and was worshiped in purifying fire rituals at open-air altars. Mazdaism was full of moral and philosophical restrictions that made human life a battle against the forces of evil. Little by little, however, the worship of Ahura Mazda became worship of the ruler. He was the King of Kings, the Master of the Universe, before whom the envoys of the twenty-eight satrapies of the empire prostrated themselves in reverence.

ALEXANDER'S DREAM

At the birth of Alexander the Great, son of Philip, king of Macedonia, a tempest was unleashed, lightning zigzagged across the sky, and two of Zeus's eagles perched on the roof of the queen's apartment. That same night, the legend continues, the Temple of Artemis at Ephesus, one of the Seven Wonders of the World, burned down. All this probably took place in October, in the year 356 B.C.

The boy was brought up in the Greek cultural tradition. He was taught gymnastics (wrestling, running, throwing, and broad jumping) to strengthen his body, music to cultivate his soul, and poetry to inspire him with a sense of glory. He found models to follow in the *Iliad* and in his hero, Achilles, from whom his mother was descended. He also learned horsemanship and hunting, a privilege of his rank. In his fourteenth year he was put in the care of Aristotle, who taught him philosophy and the sciences, instilling in him a taste for knowledge.

In 336 B.C. Philip was assassinated and Alexander became king. He began by assuming control of all the Greek states from the Danube to the Mediterranean. But his obsession, his heart's desire, and the focus of his ambitions was the conquest of Asia; this had also been his father's dream. In the spring of 335, at the head of 180 warships carrying 40,000 foot soldiers and 6,000 cavalrymen, he landed near Sigeum (now Promentory Kum Kale in Turkey). His first act was to plant his spear in the earth, as if declaring that he was taking possession of Asian soil.

Within a few months he had shaken the Persians from their position and occupied the whole of Asia Minor. He had beaten the King of Kings, Darius III, at the Battle of Issus (November 333 B.C.), occupied Tyre and Palestine, and entered Egypt. There he founded Alexandria, made sacrifices to the Egyptian gods, and had himself recognized as king of Upper and Lower Egypt, the beloved of Ammon, and son of the god Re. He then returned to Asia, where he had a further encounter with Darius's troops at Gaugamela ("The Meadow of the Camel") in 331. The spears of the Macedonian phalanx (a defensive formation) resisted the chariots of war equipped with scythe blades and stood up against the Scythian and Persian horsemen ("Aim at their faces," Alexander is said to have commanded).

Babylon and Susa were captured, Persepolis set on fire, and Darius was murdered by his own allies. Alexander pushed the limits of his conquests ever farther. He crossed the Indus and vanquished the tribes and kingdoms to the south of Kashmir, but after this his troops refused to go on.

Alexander now turned to the organization of his empire. He opened up new routes overland and by sea, and encouraged the founding of colonies, populated by soldiers, tradesmen, and the native peoples. He had a great plan to found eternal cities that would carry his name so that even today there are a number of cities from Egypt to India, such as the great metropolis of Alexandria on the Nile, that bear his name. Alexander strongly believed in the fusion of all peoples. His aim was to create a new world-society based on a common Greek culture.

But Alexander never had time to fulfill his grandiose ambitions. He died of a fever in 324 B.C. at Babylon while making plans to conquer the whole Mediterranean basin.

After Alexander's passage through Gandhara, the region saw the birth of "Greco-Buddhist" art; these two statuettes of Buddhist monks are examples of the Hellenistic influence on India. (Musée Guimet, Paris)

In early spring 329 B.C., Alexander's army continued its eastward march and, under terrible conditions, crossed the Hindu Kush, a vast mountainous barrier in the Himalayas about 13,000 feet high, between Pakistan and China.

THE MAURYAN EMPIRE OF INDIA

As soon as the news broke of Alexander's death at Babylon, several rebellions broke out in India against the Greek principalities he had left behind him. The Brahmins, members of the priestly caste, encouraged the people to throw out the "impure" foreigners, and a military chieftain, Candragupta Maurya, embarked on the conquest of the Punjab and the plains of the Ganges. In a few years, leading an army equipped with 9,000 elephants, Candragupta annexed the various kingdoms of northern India and besieged Pataliputra, capital of the state of Magadha. There, in 317 B.C., he was crowned emperor, fulfilling Alexander's dream on his own account by uniting the whole of the Indian subcontinent under one rule.

The Mauryan Empire was authoritarian, not to say despotic. The king had complete power over the army, the judiciary, legislation, and administration. However, because of its sheer size the empire had to be decentralized to some extent: it was divided into five large provinces, each administered by a governor or viceroy who was always a prince of the royal family. Before setting his seal to decrees, the king consulted two assemblies, the Council of the Town and the Council of the Kingdom—but he was free not to take their advice if he so wished. The only body to have any real influence over the king's actions was the Council of Ministers; it included the heir apparent, the Grand Chamberlain, the Supreme Military Commander, the Treasurer, the High Priest, and the Superintendent of Elephants.

The state kept a constant grip on daily life. In every town, municipal committees—which were really networks of spies—supervised industry, commerce, and foreigners. In rural areas, agricultural supervisors oversaw irrigation, the keeping of inventories, and the distribution of grain. They allocated to the king the entire production of his own estates and a quarter of that from other estates. Although the people were under this tight control, the yoke was made bearable by a certain degree of prosperity. There were two annual harvests, which produced a plentiful supply of cereals. Consequently, there was no risk of famine. In addition, the peasants were regarded as a privileged class, and their lands were protected in times of war.

At the beginning of the third century B.C. the army consisted of nearly 600,000 men, divided into three wings—the infantry, the cavalry, and the elephants. Soldiers fell into five categories: members of the warrior caste; true professional soldiers, who were reliable fighters; mercenaries recruited from the subject states; conscripts recruited for short periods; and, lastly, warriors from the forest tribes, who had few weapons but more than enough courage. Far from being on permanent campaign, the mere presence of this army enabled the king to impose his policies on his neighbors. According to the *Artha-Śāstra*, a treatise on the art of government by Candragupta's adviser Kautilya, government could take six different forms: neutrality, good understanding, alliance, deception, hostility, or total war. The skill of the ruler lay in being able to assess specific situations in order to decide whether to resort to warfare or diplomacy.

The cave temples of Ajanta were first carved in the middle of the second century B.C. Twenty-nine shrines were cut out of the rock-face, for the use of Buddhist monks during the rainy season. Pilgrims also went there to pray, and during the centuries that followed, generous benefactors had the grottos decorated with magnificent wall paintings based on the life of Buddha. With the decline of Buddhism in India, the caves were abandoned; they were only rediscovered by accident in 1819.

According to the accounts of Greek travelers, festivals at the Mauryan court at Pataliputra were lavish in the extreme. The king was carried about in a richly decorated palanquin, escorted by dancing girls, musicians, and servants leading leopards and carrying tree branches in which multicolored parrots fluttered. The royal cortege was completed by several elephants adorned in gold and silver.

ASOKA, THE BUDDHIST KING

When he ascended to the throne in 273 B.C. Candragupta's grandson, Asoka, had already had plenty of experience in ruling. He had been trained for kingship since his adolescence, had been governor of a province, and had put down a serious rebellion. According to the Buddhist chronicles, he had all his brothers and sisters murdered in order to seize the power for himself.

The empire that Asoka inherited was large and well organized. He tried to expand it even further, by carrying on his grandfather's policy of conquest. In 251 B.C. he headed a military expedition against the powerful kingdom of Kalinga, on the eastern coast of India. Both armies were large and courageous, and the fighting was merciless. On the evening of the last battle, nearly a hundred thousand bodies littered the field. Although he was the victor, Asoka was deeply disturbed by the horrors of this war. Haunted by remorse, he converted to Buddhism; he withdrew for a time to a monastery, and went on a pilgrimage to the Bodhi tree, where the Buddha had experienced enlightenment. When he returned to his capital, he decided to atone for his sins and "substitute the victory of the law for the rule of violence."

The luxury of the court was done away with, and military expenses were cut to the essential minimum. The king, henceforth known as "Deranampiya," ("the beloved of the gods") devoted himself to the welfare of his people. He had wells dug in the villages, founded hospitals, and recruited veterinarians. Throughout the empire his sayings and his laws were inscribed on pillars and rocks, inviting people to practice the "great principals of natural law"—speaking the truth, performing charitable acts, observing purity and self-control, and respecting all forms of life. Asoka also set about making the law more humane: anyone condemned to death was granted three days' respite beforehand, to allow him to prepare by fasting and praying, and giving his family time to intervene on his behalf.

The king felt it important to set a good example, and kept his subjects informed of his personal progress. Thus, an edict forbidding the sacrifice of animals was accompanied by the following statement: "In former days, in the kitchens of the king who loves the gods, thousands of animals were killed each day to be eaten; but now, at the moment when this text is being inscribed, only three animals are being killed: two peacocks and a squirrel. From now on, even these three animals will not be killed." Asoka was completely dedicated to Buddhism, and he created a new category of minister, Superintendents of the Law, who were to act as "agents of propaganda and protectors of the faithful." However, unlike many rulers in the grip of religious fervor, he permitted the practice of other religions.

Asoka died in 236 B.C. As time went by, his life story took on the character of a legend, and his reign was thought of as a "golden age" of humanity. The facts are not quite so straightforward. Although Asoka's faith was genuine, as was his desire to build an empire based on moral values, these "virtues" were still subservient to his desire for absolute power. His great achievements scarcely survived him. On his death, the empire was divided between his sons. And Buddhism was never again to hold such an important place in India.

The Edicts of Asoka were inscribed on rocks and above all on huge pillars; they are the oldest inscriptions ever found on Indian soil. Deciphering them was a difficult task. It was not until 1837 that James Prinsep, a civil servant in Benares, discovered the key to the maghadi alphabet, the official language of the Mauryan Empire. And even Asoka's name was not formally identified until 1915. On this capital of polished sandstone, four lions—today official emblems of the Republic of India—are seated over four "Wheels of the Law," symbols of the Buddhist faith, divided by a bull, a horse, an elephant, and a lion, which may represent the four points of the compass.

According to legend, Asoka was a great builder of stupas, the largest Buddhist temples, originally designed to contain the relics of the Buddha. He was supposed to have built 84,000 all over the empire, among them the Stupa of Sanchi shown here. They were originally built of brick and decorated with wood; in the first century A.D. they were rebuilt in stone.

On the evening of his victory over the powerful kingdom of Kalinga, the young king, overcome with remorse, was unable to leave the field of battle. Shortly afterward he became a Buddhist and embarked on a reign characterized by nonviolence.

THE QIN DYNASTY

Five centuries before the Christian Era, China did not exist. Its territory was divided into a multitude of small states, almost perpetually at war with one another. Each was trying to establish its own independence and expand its power at the expense of the others. The weakest of them were soon destroyed by this constant warfare and finally just seven large and well-organized kingdoms confronted each other.

Then began the period that the ancient Chinese historians called the "Warring States" (453–221 B.C.), out of which the northwestern state of Qin emerged victorious. The area was rich in good agricultural soil and also contained some large deposits of mineral ore. The Qin rulers embarked on a shrewd program of conquest, judiciously balancing brute force with the use of diplomacy. Within the kingdom itself the traditional social structure was completely changed by means of a series of reforms: the feudal system established by the Shang and Zhou Dynasties, based on the absolute power of the noble families, was replaced by a centralized system of government.

The king's policies were motivated by two major and constant preoccupations, to enrich the state and to strengthen the army. Obligatory military service was introduced, weapons and equipment were modernized, and new methods of warfare applied. The peasants, who until then had been feudally bound to the nobles, now became subjects of the king, and the merchant class pursued its activities under strict government supervision. At that time the political life of the Qin kingdom was largely directed by the Legalist philosophers, scholars who adhered to a rigid school of political thought. Shang Yang (d.338 B.C.) and particularly Han Fei (280–233 B.C.) advocated a strong state, with its power based on the law. It was their view that any means were permissible to enforce universal obedience, however coercive. The proper goal to pursue was not the happiness of the individual but the success of the state. And it was Hanfei's opinion that the subjects of the king were in any case scarcely capable of directing their own destiny. "One can no more rely on the intelligence of the people than on the mood of a baby. . . . When you lance a baby's boil it cannot understand that the small pain it suffers is the means of obtaining great relief."

In 247 B.C. Prince Zheng ascended to the Qin throne. Convinced that his kingdom's great hour had now come, he launched an out-and-out war against his rivals. In a decade of ruthless fighting, he absorbed all the neighboring states. The first to fall was the kingdom of Han, in 230 B.C., then Wei in 225, the state of Chu yielded in 223, and the Qi in 221. At this date Zheng ruled over the entire undivided territory of China. He founded an empire and took the title of Qin Shihuangdi, (First Emperor of Qin).

Qin Shihuangdi ruled over the first unified Chinese empire (Qin Dynasty) for only eleven years (221–210 B.C.). The dynasty that he had proclaimed would last for two thousand generations died out only four years after his death. Short-lived though it was, the Qin Dynasty played a fundamental role in Chinese history. It set up institutions which, despite later changes, were to remain the same for two thousand years.

An empire that was to last for two thousand generations.

From the earliest days of Chinese history, warfare was regarded as a noble occupation; it was practiced by the privileged few who owned chariots, horses, and bronze weapons. In the third century B.C. a radical change took place: men no longer fought to prove their courage or bring honor to their families, but to conquer territory. A number of manuals on strategy were produced, among them the famous Art of War by Sun Zi; and professional soldiers replaced noblemen at the head of armies. With their strong infantry and cavalry, these armies employed the most brutal methods. Mass executions were common, crops were burned, and towns and villages systematically destroyed.

During the ''Warring States'' period, Chinese bronzework was at its zenith. Beautiful objects like this Hu vase were inlaid with gold and silver. (Musée Guimet, Paris)

THE FIRST EMPEROR OF QIN

As soon as he mounted the throne, Qin Shihuangdi embarked on a mammoth project—to turn China into a great power. With this aim in mind, he applied to the empire the methods he had already found so successful in his own kingdom.

The first task was to consolidate the power, by removing the prerogatives of the nobles of the conquered states. The chief lords were executed or deported to frontier regions. Their fortunes were confiscated and some of their palaces pulled down, the materials to be reused in the building of Xianyang, the imperial capital. To ensure internal peace, every man in possession of weapons was ordered to hand them in, on pain of death. Assisted by his prime minister, Li Si, Shihuangdi divided up the government of his empire into thirty-six commands, administrative units that were each subdivided into prefectures, districts, counties, and villages. Each command had a civil governor, a military governor, and a chief of police to see that the emperor's orders were properly carried out. The penal system was strict in the extreme; it was based on the principle that if small crimes were punished with severity, people would think twice before committing larger ones. The state mercilessly hunted down anyone it considered to be idle or a social parasite. Beggars and vagrants were arrested and put right into the army or sent to work on the emperor's great collective building projects.

Shihuangdi was very preoccupied with eliminating regional differences. He unified the calendar, and brought in a single system of writing that could be read by anyone in the empire, in place of the different regional styles. A single system of weights and measures was adopted, and the axles of vehicles had to be of a standard width. Local coinages were abolished, and replaced by a universal currency of *sapeks*, round coins with a hole in the center. All this demanded a great deal of work. The imperial scribes were not allowed to take a rest until they had covered around 60 pounds of wooden writing tablets with Chinese characters!

The emperor himself was as busy as anyone; his capacity for work was legendary. Every day he read through a hundred reports, he led his troops into battle himself and fought at the northern frontier to extend his empire into Manchuria and Korea. Anxious to pass his glory on to posterity, Shihuangdi built a magnificent palace at Xianyang. A road leading to it was built for his private use, edged with high earthen banks so that no one could glimpse him passing by. Toward the end of his reign, he became haunted by a fear of death, and sent expeditions abroad in search of elixirs to prolong life. He designed his own last resting place, on a scale to match his ambitions and achievements: this gigantic mausoleum was built underground as a re-creation of the empire he had established in his lifetime; it was guarded by several thousand life-size terra-cotta (pottery) soldiers.

While on a visit to a distant province, the emperor fell ill and died. Those close to him kept his death a secret, to prevent the news from reaching Xianyang before they did. The Shihuangdi was carried back in a palanquin filled with salted herrings to mask the smell of his decaying corpse.

In 213 B.C. Qin Shihuangdi, who could not take criticism, decided to burn all the books in circulation, except for works on medicine, farming, and divination. Anyone disobeying this order was executed, including 460 scholars found guilty of protesting against the measure; the emperor ordered that they should have their hands cut off and then be buried alive.

In the afterlife the Great Emperor hoped to preserve the power he had achieved on earth. He had his tomb guarded by 6,000 terracotta soldiers, including life-size horsemen, lancers, and crossbowmen, and archers like this one, kneeling and ready to shoot. (Sian Museum)

During the ten years of the Sovereign Emperor's reign, some massive projects were carried out. Great areas of swamp were dried out, forests were cleared, and canals dug. A gigantic network of roads was built, radiating throughout the empire from the capital. Solidly built on earthen embankments, often bordered by trees, they made it easy for people and merchandise to move around the country. For the civil servants, soldiers, and merchants who used them, staging posts were set up at regular intervals.

''The king of Qin is a man with a prominent nose and large eyes, and the chest of a bird of prey; he has the voice of a jackal, the heart of a tiger or a wolf. When he is restrained, it is easy for him to seem inferior to people; when he has obtained what he wants, it is also easy for him to devour them.'' Thus wrote Sima Qian (145–86 B.C.), the first great Chinese historian. His ''historical memoirs'' are a complete collection of all the events and traditions of Chinese history since its origins. They served as a model for dozens of generations of historians.

THE GREAT WALL

The Great Wall of China has been called the Eighth Wonder of the World, and is said to be the only man-made structure that can be seen from the moon. As it stands now, it dates from the Ming Dynasty (1368–1644), but its origins go back much, much further, to the fourth century B.C., when the Warring States were still disputing the control of China. Many of the states built fortified walls at their frontiers to prevent incursions from their neighbors. For the kingdoms of the North (the Yan, Zhao, and Qin), these walls also provided protection against the menace of the nomadic Mongols of the Manchurian steppes and plains.

In 221 B.C., when Shihuangdi conquered China, anything that might impede the total unification of the new empire was systematically destroyed, starting with the ramparts that had marked the territory of the former kingdoms. But there was still the threat of the nomads. The emperor sent his chief general, Meng Tian, to the northern frontiers in order to design an effective means of keeping the barbarians out. On his return, Meng Tian proposed a colossal design: the existing walls should be kept and fortified and then linked together to form a single line of defense, about 450 miles long.

Three hundred thousand men were sent to the site. They included a good number of soldiers, as well as peasants, dismissed officials, displaced noblemen, and condemned criminals. Most would die during the work; some were buried under the wall itself, in keeping with the old belief that their life force could be passed on. The result was on a titanic scale: the 30-foot-high wall snaked across hills, following the curves of the terrain, making use of natural obstacles and passes. It was built of piled-up earth, probably covered with stone blocks and bricks. Along the top was a 23-foot-wide walkway, enabling several horsemen to patrol the frontier. Watchtowers were built into it at regular intervals, two arrow-flights apart. Each was permanently manned by a small unit of soldiers, who communicated from tower to tower by signaling with flags during the day and wood fires at night.

The Great Wall reminded the Chinese of a dragon, with its head to the east and its tail to the west. The dragon was not an evil creature but a protective goddess who symbolized vital energy. There was even a legend that the true architect of the wall was a dragon.

THE GATES OF THE GREAT WALL

This fort, in the province of Gansu, was a strategic point at the western entrance to the Great Wall of the Ming Dynasty. At an altitude of 1,960 feet, it marked the limits of the inhabited world for the caravans of the Silk Route. Beyond lay unknown territory— hostile, deserted, and haunted by demons— which they had to cross to reach their markets.

The Great Wall, begun by the Qin emperor Shihuangdi, was added to under the Hans (206–220 B.C.). It was abandoned by the Tang Dynasty (A.D. 618–907), which described it as "a monument with no strategic value." After the Mongol occupation (1276–1368), it recovered its former importance. The Ming rulers restored the entire length of it, and once more used it as the shield of China. Along its 5,486 miles, nearly a million soldiers kept watch, day and night! The Great Wall was more than a simple defensive barrier; it was a remarkable strategic route. It enabled reinforcements to travel to the farthest-flung frontiers of the empire and to ensure that they were provisioned. It also played an ecological role, since at certain points it formed a screen against the winds from the steppe, thus protecting the crops.

The only man-made structure visible from the moon.

CONFUCIUS

The most famous Chinese in history is universally known outside his native land by a Latin name. It was the Jesuit fathers in the seventeenth century who introduced his philosophy to Europe, and they who changed his name from Kongzi to Confucius.

Very little is known about the man himself. According to historical tradition, he was born in 551 B.C. to a poor but noble family in the small state of Lu, now the province of Shandong. When he had completed his studies, he wanted to join the service of the rulers of Lu. But it was a period of decadence. Throughout China, feudal society was in an explosive state, and the nobles were destroying each other in bloodthirsty combat. Confucius opened a school, and made efforts to reform the government and social behavior. Wherever he went, he reiterated: "If I could find a prince capable of using my abilities, there would be results at the end of twelve months, and perfection at the end of three years."

After many disappointments, he thought he had at last found his rightful place when the duke of Lu appointed him as an adviser. According to legend, within a few months his influence had taken effect and his reforms were bearing fruit. However, the neighboring states did not take kindly to this, afraid that under his direction the state of Lu would become too powerful. The duke of Qi cunningly sent eighty of the most beautiful singing and dancing girls to the duke of Lu, together with 120 thoroughbred horses. For the next five days the duke refused to see anyone and lost all interest in public affairs. Realizing that he no longer had the ear of the ruler, Confucius resigned from his post and left Lu. He spent the following thirteen years of his life wandering all over China, seeking in vain a ruler who would listen to his advice. Wherever he went he preached his doctrine, gathered disciples, and founded schools. In 479 B.C., at the age of seventy-two, he returned to his native land to die.

Like Socrates—with whom he was almost contemporary—Confucius left no writings. It was his disciples who wrote down the substance of his teachings in the *Analects,* a collection of a little over five hundred fragments of his conversation and sayings, written in the spoken language of the day. "I do not create, I transmit," he declared. Contrary to what is often believed, Confucianism is not a religion. It is a moral system, highly pragmatic and realistic; it emphasizes the need for an orderly social life based on existing values. Everyone must conform to his position in society and to the rules which that entails. "The prince must act as a prince, the subject as a subject, and the son as a son." In the political field, Confucius wanted to protect the social order from disruption and to entrust the power to a ruler who would be an example of moral strength and virtue. According to him, only the "educated man" or "gentleman" was a suitable person to educate the prince and inspire people with a sense of duty and respect for themselves and others. Although his thoughts have often been interpreted in contradictory ways, they were the cornerstone of Chinese civilization. Confucianism was honored during the Han Dynasty (206 B.C.–A.D. 220) and was to have a powerful influence on Chinese life for nearly twenty centuries.

Today thousands of people still visit Confucius's house, temple, and tomb at Qufu in Shandong Province.

When Confucius realized that the duke of Lu was hardly a model of virtue, he left the palace to seek a ruler more disposed to follow his advice.

Only the educated gentleman was
qualified to educate the prince.

*Tradition has it that Confucious was respon-
sible for editing the* Five Classics, *the founding texts of Chinese written culture:*

Shih ching, *or ''Classic of Poetry''*
Shu ching, *or ''Classic of History''*
I Ching, *or ''Classic of Changes''*
Li chi, *or ''Classic of Rites''*
Chiunqi, *or ''Spring and Autumn'' annals*

*Some historians believe that Confucius wrote
them himself.*
  *The purpose of these great classic texts was
to awaken man's spirit to wisdom. So one had
to know how to read them, meditate on them,
and put their teachings into practice. Large
numbers of pupils and disciples came to listen to the master's commentaries on these
works. Several centuries after his death, the
Chinese continued to venerate Confucius as
a saint. He was shown in hundreds of paintings preaching his words of wisdom, surrounded by an attentive audience.*

THE HAN CIVILIZATION

After the death of Qin Shihuangdi, the newly unified Chinese Empire fell apart again. Would-be successors jostled to claim the throne. Among them were the displaced feudal lords, anxious to reinstate their principalities, but they were successfully dealt with by Liu Bang, a minor official of peasant stock. In 206 B.C. he took the imperial throne and founded the Han Dynasty which, despite a number of serious problems, was to last for nearly four centuries. It had such a strong influence on China that even today the northern Chinese are referred to as "Han Chinese." Liu Bang, who was nicknamed Gaozu ("Great Ancestor") after his death, installed his capital at Chang'an, the modern city of Xi'an. He handed out fiefdoms and titles to his former companions in arms, but preserved the political and administrative organization set up by Shihuangdi. It is true that he relaxed some of the severest rules and regulations; punishment by mutilation, for example, was replaced by forced labor. His successors, Wendi (179–157 B.C.) and particularly Wudi (140–87 B.C.), consolidated the structure of the new state. They held regular and very accurate censuses, which enabled them to keep a tight check on individuals, and the people were subjected to a complex system of taxes, public duties, and military service. Vast portions of the population were displaced, in order to strengthen the capital and its surrounding region. A few of the ancient texts had been saved from destruction; they were returned to their place of honor, and new editions were published. An imperial university was founded in 124 B.C., and twenty-five years later the first Chinese dictionary appeared, containing 9,000 characters. At the same time, legal measures were enforced that finally ended the power of the feudal lords; a nobleman's title and lands no longer went to his first-born male heir, but were henceforth divided equally among all his sons.

Busy as they were within the kingdom, the early Hans acted with equal energy outside the Chinese frontiers. Faced with the continued threat from the Xiongnu, nomadic forebears of the Huns, Emperor Wudi pursued a resolutely warlike policy. After a dozen successful campaigns, he had swept them from his northern frontiers and was assured of the respect of his neighbors. The Chinese armies took advantage of their success by thrusting farther into Mongolia and Central Asia. At the very same time, at the other end of the continent, the envoys of the Roman Empire were moving ever farther east. Little by little the famous Silk Route became established, providing a link across deserts and mountains between the two great empires of the East and the West. In Manchuria, Korea, and even Indochina, the conquered peoples kept their own language but adopted Chinese customs and writing and a form of government that would leave its mark for centuries.

However, military expansion was an expensive game. To increase its public resources, in 119 B.C. the state imposed a monopoly on the production and sale of iron and salt. Merchants' profits were severely taxed. In the countryside, where peasants lived permanently on the brink of starvation, trouble was brewing.

The Dazzlingly Beautiful Lady

The Han emperor Yuandi (48–32 B.C.) kept a harem of 500 of the most beautiful young women in the land. Every day he chose a favorite from their portraits painted by the court artist. For a fee, the painter would make his sitters look more attractive than they really were. But one extremely beautiful woman refused to take part in this deception. The painter punished her by adding to her portrait a blemish above the right eye, which was a sign of bad luck. The emperor never picked this young woman, and for years she languished in obscurity.

In 33 B.C. Yuandi wanted to cease hostilities with the Xiongnu, and decided to offer their leader one of the beauties from his harem. In order not to deprive himself of any of his favorites, he chose to send away the one he had never seen in the flesh. He raised her to the rank of imperial princess and had her presented to him at a ceremonial audience. Overcome at the sight of her dazzling beauty, Yuandi wanted to keep her in his palace. But it was too late. The lady had to leave her native land. His sacrifice led to a long-lasting peace between the Chinese and the Xiongnu.

LUOYANG, CAPITAL OF CHINA

The site of a capital city was carefully chosen, as were all Chinese towns and cities. Priests and seers would examine the site, the nature of the soil, the direction of streams and rivers, and the shape of the local mountains. They made sure that the local deities approved of the court being established there, and checked that the five elements—water, earth, fire, wood, and metal— were in harmony with each other at the site.

Thus in A.D. 23 the Han emperor established his new capital, Luoyang. A number of years earlier, the Han power had been weakened, and a usurper, Wang Mang, had seized the opportunity to take power. But then a massive and terrible peasant revolt erupted, enabling the displaced rulers to recover the throne. To mark this new beginning, the emperor decided to leave his former capital, Chang'an, and move to Luoyang.

In keeping with tradition, Luoyang was built within a square, which the Chinese believed to be the shape of the world. The town was surrounded by a wide moat (trench) filled with water, as well as high earthen ramparts. Travelers had to enter the city through massive gateways, permanently guarded by day and closed at night. The roads were laid out in checkerboard fashion, running north-south and east-west.

The northern part of the city was the quietest, the wealthiest, and the most spacious. There stood the imperial palace, built in the middle of lush gardens and lakes. It faced south, the direction of *yang*, symbol of positive energy. Around the palace rose great temples and the houses of senior officials. The southern part of the city, by contrast, was noisy, overcrowded, and often wretched. There the buildings, made of wood, dried mud, and straw, were crowded together, with barely room between them for narrow alleyways. The city was always busy and crowded, particularly around the two big markets, which were like the city's "lungs." In all, over a million people lived in Luoyang in the first centuries of the Christian Era.

Like many other peoples, the Chinese of the Han Dynasty were buried with some of the objects they had used during their lifetime. If the objects were too bulky to put in a tomb, terracotta models were used instead. This model, found inside a tomb, gives us a very good idea of the houses in such great Chinese cities as Chang'an and Luoyang.

During the Han Dynasty a class of scholar-bureaucrats emerged. Educated in Confucianism, they managed to make themselves indispensable to the emperor in the heavy burden of governing the state. They were recruited by a system of progressive civil service examinations, which began in the provincial capitals and culminated, for the most successful candidates, at the capital. In theory, any of the emperor's subjects could enter these competitions, except for the despised professions of soldier, merchant, musician, and dancer. In fact, candidates had to find patrons among the regional officials, who would give priority to their friends and relatives. The scholar-bureaucrats enjoyed special privileges, and traveled around town in carriages attended by servants, as shown in this second-century bronze.

At dawn, a drum was beaten to announce the opening of the gates of the great city. On the banks of the Luo River hundreds of shoppers hurried to buy the cereals, vegetables, fish, and meat that were unloaded from the junks. Soldiers infiltrated the crowd to keep an eye on the activities of the craftsmen and merchants. Merchants were subject to close scrutiny; their prices were often fixed by law and their profits heavily taxed. Although they were necessary to the economy, their profession was despised. Many were not even authorized to have homes in the town, and had to live outside the ramparts.

DISCOVERIES IN CHINA

Although archaeology is a relatively recent science in the West, it has been respected in China for at least a thousand years. In the eleventh century, during the Song Dynasty, scholars and art collectors became enthralled by the ancient bronzes and jades discovered near Anyang, later identified as the last capital of the Shang Dynasty. Before these were sent to swell the contents of the royal collection, the finest pieces were examined carefully, and some of them were reproduced. And, since the art of forgery was reaching a high point, a number of copies were also made. Even better for posterity, they were listed in illustrated catalogs. *Kaogu Tu*, a meticulous inventory dating from 1092, gives the exact design, dimensions, weight, and place of origin of some 224 bronze and jade items, together with any inscriptions engraved on them.

Encouraged by educated emperors like Huizong (1101–1125), this extraordinary labor of documentation continued for some time. At the end of the twelfth century a man called Hongzun produced a catalog of ancient coins, the *Guquan*, probably the first work on numismatics (coin collecting) ever to be published.

However, from the fifteenth century onward, this interest in the past faded away. Only a few collectors bothered to assemble some of the treasures of the past on their own account. In Europe, in the nineteenth and twentieth centuries, there was a lively interest in chinoiseries, mainly in the form of paintings, lacquer work, and recently manufactured porcelain. Chinoiserie is an ornate style of decoration based on Chinese motifs.

It has only been during the past fifty years that the voice of the distant past has echoed from the depths of Chinese soil. In 1930 hundreds of tombs began to be uncovered. These dated from the Shang and Zhou periods (1766–257 B.C.) and the Han Dynasty (206 B.C.–A.D. 220). The contents of some of them have been quite extraordinary.

The jade armor of the Han princes was believed to preserve their bodies after death. Sadly, after twenty centuries of sleep under the thin jade plates laced with gold thread, only dust remained.

The Jade Prince

In 1968 a unit of the Chinese Popular Army was stationed at Mancheng, in Hebei Province. While digging out a shelter in a cliff, some soldiers discovered a long gallery cut into the mountainside. At the end was a huge funeral chamber, piled high with treasures—perfume burners, lamps, bronze vases inlaid with gold and silver. At the far end of the room lay a funeral chamber, the last resting place of Prince Liu Sheng (155–113 B.C.), one of the brothers of the great Han emperor Wudi. His wife, Du Wan, rested beside him. Both were wrapped in curious shrouds made of tiny oblong sheets of jade, linked by golden threads.

These precious wrappings reflect a major preoccupation of the ancient Chinese—to prolong survival of the body after death. Jade was regarded as a magical stone, and was rightly believed to prevent flesh from decaying. Well before the Hans, it was customary at a death to stop the openings of the body with jade amulets: jade fish were placed on the eyes, and a grasshopper over the mouth.

The Army of the Dead

In May, 1974 in the village of Xi'an in Shaanxi Province, some members of a commune who were drilling a well came across a life-size terracotta head, twelve feet down. They soon dug out a complete statue, which turned out to be that of a warrior. As this find was not far from the mound of earth covering the tomb of Qin Shihuangdi, First Emperor of China (221–210 B.C.), archaeologists were immediately sent to the site to do further research. With great care, they removed the

soil and revealed its secrets: for over two thousand years it had concealed a set of gigantic pits containing an entire army—nearly 6,000 pottery soldiers, accompanied by some magnificent horses, all life-size.

The sensational discovery of Qin Shihuangdi's mausoleum raised as many questions as it answered, starting with the authenticity of the soldiers. Some experts found it hard to believe that the First Emperor's craftsmen had managed to produce works of such exceptional sculptural quality.

And still other surprises wait for the archaeologists. There are hundreds of more tombs to exhume. The tomb of Qin Shihuangdi himself has not yet been excavated. There is an amazing description of it in the memoirs of the great historian Sima Qian (145–86 B.C.). According to this account, the interior of the tomb is an underground reproduction of the kingdom modeled on real life. The sun, moon, and stars appear, moving over a celestial vault. The sun is covered by huge bronze plates, decorated with jewels and precious objects. In the center of the necropolis is a mercury lake, with jade plants growing from it. Gold and silver birds are perched on its leaves. Lamps fueled with a special oil burn there for all eternity. And the whole

This bronze horse, discovered in Gansu Province, dates from the first century B.C. Frozen at full gallop, it is balanced by a miracle of artistry on a single hoof.

complex is surrounded by a series of traps: stones and arrows will be projected automatically to hit any intruders bold enough to enter.

Although it seems very likely that this tomb has been looted, perhaps we will know one day soon whether the ancient historian's description was accurate.

In 1974 Chinese archaeologists uncovered the remains of an underground construction 1,435 yards square. They found themselves in the presence of one of the most astonishing discoveries of the twentieth century: 6,000 clay warriors, 5 feet 8 inches tall on average, carrying bows and arrows, knives, spears, and crossbows. They were arranged in strict battle order, with a 72-column advance guard, a 38-column corps, two flanks, and a rear guard. Beside them were life-size horses led by grooms or harnessed in fours to chariots. This gigantic army is part of the mausoleum of the first Chinese emperor, Qin Shihuangdi (221–210 B.C.). The mausoleum was designed as a subterranean reproduction of the world of the living. The excavations have not yet been completed, but it is fairly certain that further suprises await the researchers. (Xi'an Museum)

TUTANKHAMEN

The warm air escaping from the chamber made the candle flame flicker. But as the man's eyes grew accustomed to the light, the details of the room seemed to emerge slowly from the shadows: "strange animals, statues and gold—everywhere the glint of gold." For a moment he stood still in stunned amazement. Thus the English archaeologist Howard Carter at last made the most exciting discovery of modern archaeology—the royal tomb of Tutankhamen, found intact in 1922 after 3,200 years of oblivion.

Tutankhamen's gold funeral mask is a genuine masterpiece, inlaid with lapis lazuli, turquoise, moonstone, and carnelian and covered with vitreous paste. Inside, an inscription appeals to all the gods to allow the pharaoh to "triumph over the night" and "be reborn to eternal day." (Cairo Museum)

An unknown young pharaoh

About 400 miles south from Cairo is the rocky site of Biban el Muluk, better known as the Valley of the Kings. Its high limestone cliffs shelter the tombs of the New Kingdom pharaohs (1567–1085 B.C.). These tombs were hewn from the rockface itself. In 1907, Carter began to excavate all the sections of this vast necropolis that had not yet been explored.

Carter's ambitious project was backed by Lord Carnarvon, a rich and enlightened British collector and art patron. He was passionately interested in Egyptian archaeology, and provided Carter with the funds and support he needed for nearly fifteen years.

Every winter between 1907 and 1922 Carter went to Egypt to work on the excavation. He possessed a detailed record of the sites already excavated and worked tirelessly, following a minutely charted

The tomb, discovered in November, 1922, was filled with rubble and was quite difficult to clear. Carter was not able to open the great stone sarcophagus for several months. It contained three inlaid coffins, one inside the other, the innermost one of solid gold. Inside lay the royal remains, wrapped in linen bandages, with protective amulets inserted between the layers.

plan, moving systematically from one untouched area to the next. His hope was to find the tomb of a little known sovereign of the Eighteenth Dynasty, who reigned— according to a few ancient inscriptions— between Akhenaten, the heretic king, and Horemheb, the last ruler of the Eighteenth Dynasty. The years went by. Carter remained optimistic, but Lord Carnarvon's money was running out. During the summer of 1922, Carnarvon told Carter that unless he produced some positive results he would have to withdraw his support. Carter, in despair, pleaded with him: there was only one small triangle of land left to explore! Carnarvon gave him one last chance. All Carter's hopes were fixed on that tiny piece of land. Nearby, the foundations of some ancient huts had been uncovered, which must have been used by the necropolis work force. It seemed very unlikely that a royal tomb would have been built so close to these—but Carter owed it to himself to play this one last card.

In October 1922 the improbable happened: Carter and his workers discovered a tiny staircase hollowed out in the rock, followed by a series of sealed doors. The tomb was intact! Feverishly, Carter deciphered the royal names on the seals. They were indeed those of the mysterious Eighteenth Dynasty pharaoh, Tutankhamen.

Carter called Carnarvon, who was staying in Egypt at the time. Together, they broke the seals, entered the vault, discovered its treasures, and unveiled its secrets—statues, furniture of precious woods, alabaster vases, painted funeral boats, ebony coffers inlaid with ivory, piles of jewels, a royal chariot in gold-plated wood, weapons decorated with inlaid designs, and musical instruments. The sarcophagus, or stone coffin, of the young king containing the precious mummy was covered with a golden mask, a portrait of the king. It took Carter eight more years of excavation to uncover everything contained in that royal tomb!

The "curse" of Tutankhamen

Such an important discovery was bound to arouse some bad feelings in the Service of Antiquities, an organization founded by the French in the nineteenth century when they were in sole charge of excavations on Egyptian soil.

Very soon, Carter and Carnarvon were plagued by troubles—first in the form of administrative delays, and then by political problems. Up until then Egypt had been under British protection, but in 1918 a strong nationalist movement had begun to emerge and British troops were withdrawn in 1922. The newly independent Egypt wanted to express its power and preserve its cultural heritage from the officially sanctioned pillage that it had undergone from both the British and the French.

It was out of the question for Carnarvon to take away a large part of the treasure to cover his expenses; the government felt entitled to first pick. In any case, Carnarvon scarcely had time, for in 1923 he died in Cairo of a highly mysterious illness. The story went that in his delirium the unfortunate nobleman believed he was struggling with a bird that tore at his face. Inevitably, people thought of the Egyptian funeral text which said that a curse in the form of a bird would fall on anyone who profaned a tomb. During the following years, a remarkable series of deaths occurred among Carter's colleagues, all of them adding credence to the legend of the curse.

Since then, many explanations have been offered for the disasters. One of the most recent suggestions is that there was a kind of poisonous fungus growing in the tombs and that this fungus produced severe inflammation of the respiratory tract.

In 1930 Carter finished excavating the royal tomb. In that same year the Egyptian government passed a law forbidding the removal of the objects it contained. Egypt would keep its treasure.

When they learned about all this wealth assembled in honor of a politically unimportant pharaoh who had reigned only a short time, people began to have ideas about the tombs of the great Egyptian pharaohs—Ramses and Thutmose. And these, too, suffered from looting.

This 6-foot-tall redwood statue, covered in bitumen and gold on plaster, represents the king's Ka, the part of the human personality that lives on after death. (Cairo Museum)

71

THE SEVEN WONDERS OF THE WORLD

Certain works of sculpture and architecture were admired by all the people of antiquity. They symbolized the height of artistic achievement of the Mediterranean world. In the third century, a Greek writer, Philo of Byzantium, devoted a work to them, naming them for the first time "The Seven Wonders of the World."

The seven were the mausoleum at Halicarnassus, the lighthouse at Alexandria, the Colossus of Rhodes, the statue of Zeus at Olympia, the Temple of Artemis at Ephesus, the Great Pyramid of Khufu at Giza, and the Hanging Gardens of Babylon. With the exception of the last two, all were Greek.

Only one still stands today, and that, paradoxically, is the oldest. Built around 2800 B.C. the Great Pyramid of Khufu still rises triumphantly on the edge of the Libyan Desert. The people of antiquity called it "Hakuit" ("The Luminous One") because of the reflective quality of its limestone facing. It has defied both time and humanity, since no one has yet explained satisfactorily how its gigantic blocks were put together.

In Babylon, Alexander's soldiers were impressed by the Hanging Gardens when he seized the city in 331 B.C. According to an inaccurate Greek tradition, they were the creation of Semiramis, the legendary queen of Assyria. In actual fact it was King Nebuchadrezzar who had them built in the sixth century B.C. to give pleasure to his wife Amytis, daughter of the king of the Medes. Condemned to live in the flat countryside of Babylon, the exiled princess was reminded of the wooded mountains of her homeland by these high, leafy terraces.

From dream to reality: the Colossus of Rhodes as imagined by Abraham Storck in the seventeeth century (Municipal Museum of Mâcon), and all that remains today of the temple of Zeus at Olympia, where Phidias's magnificent chryselephantine statue of the god stood.

Immortal and ephemeral

During the second half of the fourth century B.C., Artemisia II, queen of Caria, had a magnificent tomb built in the town of Halicarnassus in memory of her husband, Mausolus. In the days of Augustus's great architect, Vitruvius, the walls were still

The three great pyramids of Giza as imagined by a fifteenth-century artist, probably from a traveler's exaggerated description.

"very fine and very complete, and covered in a dressing so highly polished that it resembles glass." All that is left of this building today is a fragment bearing the single word "Mausoleum."

Neither is anything left of the great white lighthouse built on the Pharos peninsula, at the entrance to the port of Alexandria. It was designed by the architect Sostratus of Cnidos, in the reign of the Greek king Ptolemy Philadelphus around 285 B.C. Nearly three centuries later, Pliny the Elder was still writing in praise of the great tower, with its lights that signaled ships safely into harbor at night.

In 304 B.C. the island of Rhodes gallantly resisted the onslaughts of the Macedonian king Demetrius Poliorcetes, "the Besieger." The victorious city commemorated the event by putting a colossal statue of Helios, the sun god and protector of Rhodes up in the entrance to its port. It was the work of the sculptor Chares of Lindos. It has been described as anywhere from 89 to 105 feet high. Some drawings made by travelers during the Middle Ages show that in those days it still stood at the entrance to the port. But by then it was in pieces. In the first century, the Greek geographer Strabo wrote that it had fallen, broken at the knees, as the result of an earthquake.

The great Athenian sculptor Phidias made the famous statue of Zeus at Olympia. It was about 36 feet high, and was chryselephantine—that is, made of gold (*khrusos*) and ivory (*elephantos*). Its splendor made Phidias famous throughout the ancient world.

Another example of Greek genius was the temple of Artemis at Ephesus. According to the Roman writer Pliny, "It took the whole of Asia twenty years to build it." Designed by the architect Chirocrates in the fourth century B.C., it was built on marshland to ensure that it could not be destroyed by earthquakes. It represents a significant achievement in architectural balance. Pliny writes that the crosspiece over the door (the lintel) was so heavy that the architect was near suicide, despairing of ever being able to have it lifted into place! But during his sleep the goddess Artemis appeared to him to reassure him, and placed the massive stone in position herself. The temple of Artemis was completed in the second half of the third century B.C., and was celebrated throughout the Greek world. But in A.D. 263 it was looted and burned down by bands of Goths. It was restored, but later destroyed once and for all as a pagan temple.

Some ancient texts add two more wonders to these seven. While more recent in construction, they are also quite outstanding. These are the monumental altar to Zeus at Pergamum, and the temple at Epidaurus, dedicated to Asclepius, Greek god of medicine and healing, where sick people flocked in the hope of a cure.

Pyramides Aegypti.

PLUNDERING THE PAST

Very often several thousand years stand between us and the objects of the ancient world. It's an idea we have become used to since archaeology has filled the museums of the world with these ever more ancient pieces of historical evidence. And yet the fact that many of these precious articles, statues, and monuments have survived relatively intact over all these centuries is something of a miracle. Of course, what we have today represents only a fraction of what once existed. In addition to the ravages of time and warfare, the riches of the past have been systematically looted.

Looting has existed since the days of antiquity. In Egypt a papyrus dating from the Ramesside period (reign of Ramses III–XI) relates how the guardians of the Valley of the Kings turned a blind eye to tomb robbers. In his writings the Roman Cicero (106–43 B.C.) denounced, more than once, the behavior of Caius Verrus, proconsul of Sicily, who maintained a band of temple robbers, solely for the purpose of acquiring their treasures for himself. And, far from being the work of a few isolated individuals, looting was also one of the traditional acts of war. After their conquest of Egypt, the Romans appropriated several obelisks, which they used to decorate the *spinae*, the walls dividing the racetracks in Roman hippodromes. In the same fashion, the future dictator Sulla, during his Greek campaign (87–86 B.C.), filled whole ships with statues and took them home to Italy.

French soldiers taking part in a treasure hunt in Crete at the beginning of the twentieth century, when modern archaeology was just beginning.

It was shortly after midday on the 24th of August A.D. 79. A black cloud in the shape of a tall pine arose from the top of Mt. Vesuvius. Soon a city at the foot of the mountain was plunged into darkness under a hail of ash and streams of seething water. Three days later the sun shone out over the ruined city. Pompeii, once a flourishing and splendid city second only to Rome, lay under a layer of lava some 20 to 23 feet deep.

Through the centuries, Pompeii lay forgotten. It was not until 1748 that the excavation began. It was to be the longest and greatest archaelogical exploration of any part of the ancient world.

The unearthing of Pompeii had revealed a city frozen in time. Though it is not known how many people perished, more than 2,000 skeletons have already

It was not long before pillage become a commercial enterprise. In the sixteenth century court of the French king Francis I ''mummy powder'' was exchanged for gold for its supposed aphrodisiac and rejuvenating qualities. This trade was organized by the merchants of Cairo and Alexandria, in league with peasants who dug up mummies wherever they could find them to extract the precious powder. During the reign of Louis XIV (1643–1715) it was still being sold at outrageous prices.

In the seventeenth century, people became interested in the Orient and ''antiquities.'' European travelers were fascinated by the mysterious inscriptions on ancient carvings and brought back all kinds of treasures, including statuettes, seals, and amulets. They were often kept in private houses in ''curio cabinets.''

Little by little the nations of Europe became aware that these remnants of the past had a lot to teach them about their own history. The marvels of Greece, Egypt, and Italy became much admired. Moreover, Europeans saw themselves as the natural inheritors of these cultures. In the nineteenth century the first scientific expeditions were organized with the purpose of bringing back as many antiquities as possible to fill the museums. This type of pillage had official sanction, but it took place in an atmosphere of ferocious competition.

been found in the ruins. Archaeologists have recreated the very shapes of the victims by pouring liquid plaster into the hollows left by the bodies when they decomposed. The casts of these victims recreate the drama of the catastrophe. We see the cast of a mule driver crouching down by a wall in a vain attempt to escape by shielding himself with his cloak against the falling ash. The mule was also found not very far away. Buildings and works of art have also been remarkably preserved. Even paintings have all the vividness of their original colors.

The excavations at Pompeii have revealed vital information about the social, economic, political, and religious life of the period. But the work is far from complete. About one fourth of it remains to be excavated.

TREASURE HUNTING

In 1843 a Frenchman, Prisse d'Avennes, who had lived in Egypt for a long time, heard that a Prussian expedition led by Karl Richard Lepsius was on its way to Egypt from Berlin. The purpose of the expedition was to procure a set of bas-reliefs from Karnak for the German royal collection. Prisse d'Avennes already had an interest in this monument. He hurried there, hastily removed the carvings, and loaded them onto his ship to take them to Alexandria and then to France. On the way back, he passed the Prussian boats on the Nile, and couldn't resist inviting his unlucky rival to coffee aboard his ship!

When they gained their independence, Egypt and Greece made a determined effort to stem the flow of their treasures abroad. They imposed harsh laws on archaeologists, allowing them to make studies on the spot but forbidding them to take anything away. But illegal looting continued to flourish. Between 1945 and 1975, nearly 42,000 stolen items were retrieved by international search organizations. Italy has been the most highly looted coun-

The market in antiquities still creates a lucrative traffic in the products of tomb robbing. "Mummy powder" may have lost its reputation as an aphrodisiac, but the objects found in Egyptian tombs are sought after by private collectors.

try in Europe; it is estimated that between 30 and 40 percent of the excavations there have been illegal. The fate of the Latin American sites has been even more dramatic. Existing in large numbers, and badly guarded, they have been systematically looted by organized bands who provide the largest part of the world market in antiquities. In Costa Rica about 1 percent of the entire working population is engaged in the traffic in pre-Columbian art objects!

CHRONOLOGY

	Egypt	Asia Minor and Mesopotamia	India and China

-3000	3200 Narmer founds the 1st dynasty
	2780–2280 Old Kingdom
	  (3rd–6th dynasties)
	  Capital: Memphis		

-2500	Pyramids and Sphinx of Giza (4th dynasty)
	2280–2052 1st Intermediate Period
	  (7th–6th dynasties)
		Assyrian trading stations in Anatolia
		
		Hittite migrations
			2500–1500 Indus Civilization
			  Cities of Harappa and Mohenjo-Daro

-2000	**2052–1778 Middle Kingdom**
	  (12th dynasty)
	  Sesostris III (1887–1849)
	1778–1567 2nd Intermediate Period
	  (13th–17th dynasties)
	  Hyksos invasions
		1760 Hammurabi, King of Babylon
		
		1680–1200 Hittite Empire
			1766–1112 Shang Dynasty in China

-1500	**1567–1085 New Kingdom**
	  (18th–22nd dynasties)
	  Capital: Thebes
	  Thutmosis III (1504–1450)
	  Amenophis IV (Akhenaton) (1379–1362)
	  Ramses II (1304–1237)
		Capital: Hattushash
		  Suppiliuliuma (1380–1336)
		
		1284 Egypto-Hittite treaty
		1244–609 Assyrian Empire
		  Capital: Nineveh
		  Tukulti-Ninurta I (1244–1208)
		  Sargon II (721–705)
			1112–257 Zhou Dynasty in China

-1000	1085–715 3rd Intermediate Period
	  (21st–24th dynasties)
	  Capitals: Thebes (south)
	         Tanis (north)
	715–330 Late Period
	  (25th–30th dynasties)
	  Psammetichus I (663–610)
	  Nechao (610–594)
	675 Assyrian Conquest
		Sennacherib (704–681)
		  Assurbanipal (688–627)
		
		625–539 Neo-Babylonian Empire
		  Capital: Babylon
		  Nabopolassar (625–605)
		  Nebuchadrezzar II (604–562)
			563 Presumed birth of Buddha
			551 Presumed birth of Confucius

-500	529 Persian conquest
	
	332 Conquest by Alexander the Great
	330–31 Ptolemaic (Greek) Period
	  Ptolemaic Dynasties
	  Capital: Alexandria
	  Cleopatra (51–30)
		539–331 Persian Empire
		  Capitals: Pasargadae
		         Persepolis
		  Darius I (522–486)
		331–324 Empire of Alexander (356–324)
			453–221 The Warring States of China
			
			Alexander's conquests in India
			317–185 Mauryan Empire
			  Capital: Pataliputra
			  Chandragupta (317–297)
			  Asoka (273–236)
			221 1st Chinese Empire
			  Capital: Xianyang
			  Qin Shihuangdi (221–210)
			206 B.C.–220 A.D.
			  Han Dynasty
			  Capitals: Chang'an
			         Luoyang

	31 Roman Conquest		

Further Reading

The Age of God Kings: Time Frame 3000–1500 B.C. by the Editors of Time-Life Books, Time-Life Books, 1987.

Atlas of Ancient Egypt by John Baines and Jaromir Málek, Facts on File, 1980.

Atlas of the Greek World by Peter Levi, Facts on File, 1981.

Atlas of the Roman World by Tim Cornell and John Matthews, Facts on File, 1982.

Barbarian Tides: Time Frame 1500–600 B.C. by the Editors of Time-Life Books, Time-Life Books, 1987.

Cultural Atlas of China by Caroline Blunden and Mark Elvin, Facts on File, 1983.

Empires Ascendant: Time-Frame 400 B.C.–200 A.D. by the Editors of Time-Life Books, Time-Life Books, 1988.

A Soaring Spirit: Time Frame 600–400 B.C. by the Editors of Time-Life Books, Time-Life Books, 1987.

INDEX

The head of Ramses II at Luxor.

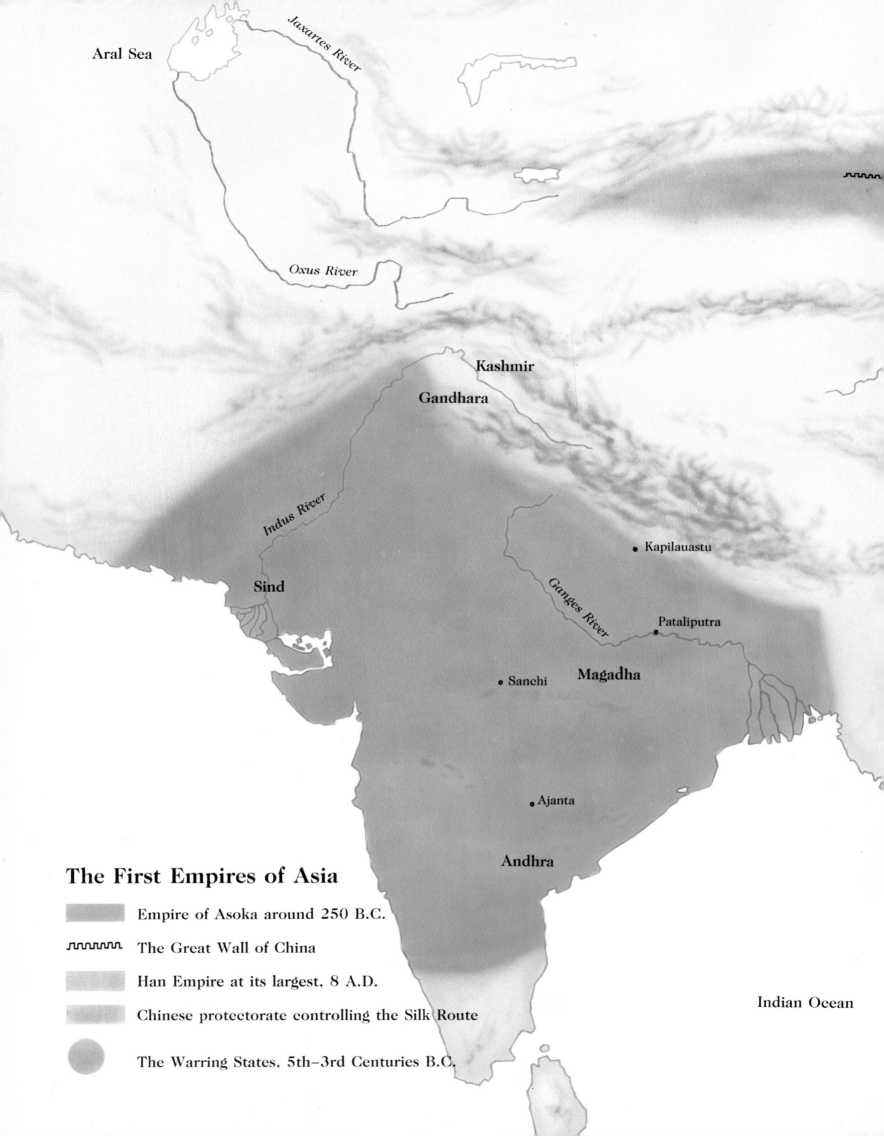

Aral Sea

Jaxartes River

Oxus River

Kashmir

Gandhara

Indus River

Kapilauastu

Sind

Ganges River

Pataliputra

Sanchi

Magadha

Ajanta

Andhra

The First Empires of Asia

Empire of Asoka around 250 B.C.

The Great Wall of China

Han Empire at its largest, 8 A.D.

Chinese protectorate controlling the Silk Route

The Warring States, 5th–3rd Centuries B.C.

Indian Ocean